"Is the church ready to listen to the voices from #MeToo? With the biblical story of Babel as the metanarrative, Li Ma's careful multidisciplinary analysis reveals dangerous, subversive patterns, which include devaluing women and making idols of power and influence. She brings her own unique global perspective to this work, noting how these Western patterns have influenced the church worldwide. The results are disastrous, on display publicly in numerous scandals of moral leadership failure, including #MeToo and #ChurchToo. The antidote according to Li Ma is found in Philippians 2, where Jesus, who holds all power, shows us a revolutionary way to use it."

—**Bonnie Nicholas**, Director, Safe Church Ministries

"Li Ma has developed a powerful and compelling critique of the celebrityism and other maladies that afflict a twenty-first-century American evangelicalism more indebted to Hollywood than the cross. Her searing analysis made me sit upright, especially because what happens in American evangelicalism has such profound effect, for good and for ill, on global Christianity. Read her to the very end where the redemptive hope of the cross shines brightly over our Babelian muck and mire."

—**Robert Osburn**, Founder and President, Wilberforce Academy

"In this insightful book Li Ma uses the Babel story to illustrate the way people rely on their own entrepreneurial designs rather than trusting in God's gracious purposes. Providing us with a careful survey of the present-day church scene, she points to the ways in which many evangelical churches seek growth, cultural relevance, and even political influence, by employing entrepreneurial strategies that serve as substitutes for promoting faithful discipleship."

—**Richard J. Mouw**, President Emeritus, Fuller Theological Seminary

"Using the tower of Babel story as a frame, Li Ma shows how the desire for growth, influence, and fame in the evangelical church, both in the US and around the world, has led to scandals and the subversion of Christianity. Using an interdisciplinary approach, she analyzes in detail the televangelism movement, the megachurch movement, the Promise Keepers movement, and the new-Calvinist movement. What makes her discussion of these developments stand out from others is her creative exegesis, the richness of her multidisciplinary analysis, and the vast range of her references. An informative and illuminating read!"

—**Nicholas Wolterstorff**, Noah Porter Professor Emeritus of Philosophical Theology, Yale University, author of *Justice: Rights and Wrongs*

"For anyone navigating the cultural thicket of American Christianity, Li Ma provides both incisive critical analysis and a way forward in hope. This book's strength lies not only in its prophetic lament and pastoral wisdom but also in its sure-footed interdisciplinary scholarship. Readers will find a deeper understanding of the problems that beset the church today and a more expansive vision of Christian faith for tomorrow."

—**Peter Choi**, author of *George Whitefield: Evangelist for God and Empire*

"Li Ma's *Babel Church* is a well-researched, cogent exegesis of the American church's marriage to 'bigger is better.' She highlights the stark contrast between God's surprising upside-down kingdom and today's corporate church structures that celebrate celebrity and marginalize the broken. A must-read for people who love the church and want to see her build the kingdom in Spirit-led, winsome ways."

—**Mary DeMuth**, author of *We Too: How the Church Can Respond Redemptively to the Sexual Abuse Crisis*

"Li Ma examines the biblical story of the tower of Babel and applies its lens to the modern church, especially the evangelical movements that have adopted mass media to spread globally. It's hardly surprising that these have become addicted to image, fame, and power. As Genesis warns, their toppling is not only inevitable, but necessary. Examining abuses of power—with a particular eye on #MeToo scandals—*Babel Church* is packed with scriptural references, including many that interpret Jesus's crucifixion. Ma does not linger long on any one figure, tradition, or story, but ignites a sense of urgency. Cautioning against vainglory and its consequences, *Babel Church* calls the church to a humbler stance, clearer sight, and prophetic speech."

—**Ruth Everhart**, author of *Ruined* and *The #MeToo Reckoning: Facing the Church's Complicity in Sexual Abuse and Misconduct*

"Li Ma has done Christianity a great service by exposing the dark side of modern evangelicalism's mode of operations. Drawing from an impressive array of cross-disciplinary scholarship, she reveals how the underlying North American evangelical system has more in common with fallen Babel rather than with Jesus and his kingdom. Tracing various evangelical movements, such as televangelists; megachurches; the young, reformed, and restless, including the global manifestations beyond North America, Li Ma's grim diagnosis of evangelicalism is a must-read for anyone who wants to better understand how modern evangelicalism has fallen into systemic abuses of power. We will do well to heed Li Ma's prescription for the cures."

—**Shiao Chong**, Editor-in-Chief, *The Banner* magazine

"Li Ma keenly understands the fault lines and pitfalls of American-style Christianity and the besetting sins of too many American churches and media empires. But what makes this book compelling is her deep insight into how this unhappy state of affairs has been exported abroad and where it has shown up as corruptions of churches around the world. Much of what Ma conveys here is sorrowful to consider. But all of it is vital to understand."

—**Scott Hoezee**, Director, The Center for Excellence in Preaching, Calvin Theological Seminary

Babel Church

Babel Church

The Subversion of Christianity in an Age of Mass Media, Globalization, and #MeToo

Li Ma

CASCADE Books • Eugene, Oregon

BABEL CHURCH
The Subversion of Christianity in an Age of Mass Media, Globalization, and #MeToo

Copyright © 2021 Li Ma. All rights reserved. Except for brief quotations in critical publications or reviews, no part of this book may be reproduced in any manner without prior written permission from the publisher. Write: Permissions, Wipf and Stock Publishers, 199 W. 8th Ave., Suite 3, Eugene, OR 97401.

Cascade Books
An Imprint of Wipf and Stock Publishers
199 W. 8th Ave., Suite 3
Eugene, OR 97401

www.wipfandstock.com

PAPERBACK ISBN: 978-1-7252-6861-6
HARDCOVER ISBN: 978-1-7252-6860-9
EBOOK ISBN: 978-1-7252-6862-3

Cataloguing-in-Publication data:

Names: Ma, Li, author.

Title: Babel church: the subversion of Christianity in an age of mass media, globalization, and #metoo / by Li Ma.

Description: Eugene, OR: Cascade Books, 2021 | Includes bibliographical references and index.

Identifiers: ISBN 978-1-7252-6861-6 (paperback) | ISBN 978-1-7252-6860-9 (hardcover) | ISBN 978-1-7252-6862-3 (ebook)

Subjects: LCSH: Church renewal. | Mass media in religion—United States. | Evangelicalism—United States. | Christianity and culture—China.

Classification: BV652.97.U6 (print) | BV652 (ebook)

03/12/21

For Mingdong Paul Lee,
Emily Brink,
and Jinny DeJoung,
whose Christ-like humility
and selfless servanthood
inspired me to battle on.

Contents

Acknowledgments | ix

Chapter 1: Introduction | 3
Chapter 2: Technique and Entrepreneurism | 22
Chapter 3: Media and Reputational Capital | 42
Chapter 4: Engineering a Movement | 58
Chapter 5: Scandalous Confusion | 75
Chapter 6: Global Epidemic | 95
Chapter 7: The Antidote: Philippians 2:5–8 | 119
Epilogue | 137

Bibliography | 141
Index | 161

Acknowledgments

I felt the need to write this book after the publication of an earlier research monograph entitled *Religious Entrepreneurism in China's Urban Churches* (Routledge, 2019). Due to its length limitations given by the publisher, I saved some theological reflections for a later project. People who knew me and my research would probably realize that I had more to say. Thus this book. So in a sense, *Babel Church* is a sequel volume. Interested readers may put these two books side by side to understand what I am trying to spell out.

I am indebted to many people who have not just supported and encouraged me, but also read parts or the entirety of the manuscript. My thanks go to colleagues, mentors and friends including Michael Barablas, Casey Jen, Steve De Vries, Al Gelder, Arie Leder, Wayne TenHarmsel, and many others. This book is dedicated to three spiritual mentors in my life: Mingdong Paul Lee, Emily Brink, and Jinny DeJong. They have modeled Christ-like humility and selfless servanthood to me. When spiritual battles become intense, I am reminded by their examples that there are people who have lived out their integrity and authenticity as Christian leaders in this tempting world. It is truly rewarding to be in their company.

My special thanks to Harriette Mostert who kindly helped with editing the manuscript. She has always provided encouragement to me. This book would not exist without the support of my husband, Jin Li, who has always believed that it is worthwhile. I am also grateful to be encouraged by Michael Thompson, who I had the pleasure to meet up with in Grand Rapids, and other editors at Cascade who helped with the publication of this book.

Finally, my gratitude to survivors and advocates of the #MeToo and #ChurchToo movements who remain an inspiration to me.

Li Ma

Grand Rapids, Michigan

Christians and the church have wanted an alliance with everything that represents power in the world. In reality this rests on the conviction that thanks to the power of the Holy Spirit the powers of this world have been vanquished and set in service of the gospel, the church, and mission. We must use their forces in the interest of evangelism. . . . But what happens is the exact opposite.
—Jacques Ellul, *The Subversion of Christianity*

The long painful history of the Church is the history of people ever and again tempted to choose power over love, control over the cross, being a leader over being led. Those who resisted this temptation to the end and thereby give us hope are the true saints.
—Henri Nouwen, *In the Name of Jesus*

Chapter 1

Introduction

The 2006 movie *Babel* is a masterwork, weaving together plots of American, Moroccan, Mexican, and Japanese stories. It presents the tragic futility of human communication across racial, socioeconomic, and cultural barriers. But very few reviewers have commented on another important theme, that of American privilege in an age of globalization, the fact that American citizens' circumstances and safety concerns may induce a butterfly effect, upsetting the life chances of people inhabiting other parts of the world.[1]

The downstream effect of American privilege is also evident when looking at the spread of Protestant missions in today's world. As two North American authors of *Geography of Grace* write self-critically, "our proclamation of the gospel is often a product of the power and privileges we enjoy."[2] The result is often one of mixed blessings to other parts of the world.

Last year I had a discussion with a conscientious American missionary friend, Bob (a pseudonym), about leadership failures in the Chinese church. He speaks fluent Mandarin Chinese and has worked for many years mentoring Chinese church leaders. After hearing my thoughts on how celebrity worship and power abuse had harmed local faith communities in China, Bob said, "To clear the murky water in the downstream, we need to go to the upstream and stop the pollution there." I knew that by "upstream" he was referring to the root cause. But I then uttered to him something that surprised us both: "But Bob, you are the upstream. You Americans brought that church model to us." Fortunately, my American friend was not offended, and

---

1. The term "butterfly effect" comes from chaos theory, referring to how small changes in initial conditions might incur changes that have a great impact on the larger state of a system.
2. Rocke and Van Dyke, *Geography of Grace*, 19.

we eventually entered into a deeper reflection on the contagious spread of trendy but deceptive ministry models from the United States to other parts of the world. This book is a direct result of that conversation.

In 1995, American historian Mark Noll published *The Scandal of the Evangelical Mind*, reminding evangelicals of their failure in "sustaining serious intellectual life."[3] Noll also states that "the evangelical ethos is activistic, populist, pragmatic, and utilitarian. It allows little space for broader or deeper intellectual effort because it is dominated by the urgencies of the moment."[4] A decade later, Canadian-born American theologian Ronald Sider wrote equally critical words about the evangelical conscience and conduct: "Scandalous behavior is rapidly destroying American Christianity. By their daily activity, most 'Christians' regularly commit treason. With their mouths they claim that Jesus is Lord, but with their actions they demonstrate allegiance to money, sex, and self-fulfillment."[5] In 2016, American political scientist Corwin Smidt wrote that "Americans are far less likely today than several decades ago to rate the honesty and ethical standards for clergy highly. . . . [A]s a group, their collective standing has diminished."[6] By 2019, what was left of the moral backbone of American evangelicalism has been broken almost completely both by the pervasive sexual abuse as exposed by the #MeToo movement and by wholesale buy-in of a radical right-wing political agenda in the name of Trumpism. Evangelicalism is leaving not just a scandalous but a traumatic mark on public life. Furthermore, psychologist Diane Langberg comments that "trauma is the mission field of our time."[7]

Meanwhile, globalization of American evangelicalism has also produced bad fruits in other parts of the world, including in the fastest growing Christian presence in continents such as Africa and Asia.[8] How has

---

3. Noll, *Scandal of the Evangelical Mind*, 3. With regard to the definition of "evangelical," see scholars such as George Marsden, David Bebbington, Mark Noll, and Frances FitzGerald, who define "evangelicals" as a group sharing the following characteristics: biblicism, conversionism, activism, crucicentrism. Admittedly, there are also scholars who dispute that when it comes to American evangelicalism, these distinctives might not capture the whole picture. See Marsden, *Understanding Fundamentalism and Evangelicalism*; Bebbington, *Evangelicalism in Modern Britain*; Noll, *Rise of Evangelicalism*; FitzGerald, *Evangelicals*.

4. Noll, *Scandal of the Evangelical Mind*, 3.

5. Sider, *Scandal of the Evangelical Conscience*, 12–13.

6. Smidt, *Pastors and Public Life*, 206.

7. Langberg, quoted in Monroe, "Must Read."

8. Wong, "Inside Singapore's City Harvest." Mtshilibe, "Fake Pastors and False Prophets." Sang-Hun, "South Korean Church Leader Sentenced." Bell, "Biggest Megachurch on

INTRODUCTION

contemporary evangelicalism come to this dramatic stage of subversion? What has gone wrong? Is there any hope? These are the main questions I want to explore in this book.

The Alarm Bell of #MeToo

As the second decade of the twenty-first century draws to a close, the issues of Christian hypocrisy are not just found in the rising divorce rates, materialism, and the neglect of a biblical worldview, but something much worse—systemic sexual abuse of the most vulnerable (women and children) and subsequent cover-ups in evangelical churches, known as the #MeToo and #ChurchToo movements.[9] A brief review of news headlines brings out this devastating reality—a sexual abuse epidemic that has affected some of the most well-known pastors and congregations, presenting the worst possible deviation from the love and truth that the Christian gospel proclaims.

- "Inside the Investigation into Child Sexual Abuse at Sovereign Grace Ministries," *Time* magazine, February 16, 2016
- "Rachael Denhollander Discusses Sovereign Grace Scandal on The Story with Martha Maccalum," *Fox News*, March 16, 2018
- "#ChurchToo: Andy Savage Resigns from Megachurch over Past Abuse," *Christianity Today*, March 20, 2018
- "Megachurch Pastor Bill Hybels Resigns from Willow Creek after Women Allege Misconduct," *The Washington Post*, April 11, 2018
- "Silence Is Not Spiritual: The Evangelical #MeToo Movement," *The New Yorker*, June 15, 2018

Earth."

9. The phrase "#MeToo" was first established on social media in 2006 by some sexual harassment survivors and activists. In 2017, following the exposure of sexual abuse allegations against Hollywood producer Harvey Weinstein, American actress Alyssa Milano called for all women who have experienced sexual abuse to write "Me too" on Twitter, leading to millions of women speaking out. In 2019, the movement gave way to the #ChurchToo trend with media coverage of sexual abuses within American Protestant churches. The word *systemic* is related to a whole system or structure, usually on local levels. Systemic abuse, not necessarily large in percentage, is caused by the erosion of every structural element that sustains the organism of a social entity, especially structures that are supposed to protect the abused.

5

- "#ChurchToo: Evangelical Leaders' Warning about the Widespread Problem of Sexual Abuse," *CBN News*, September 20, 2018
- "Al Mohler Is Apologizing for Supporting Former Sovereign Grace Leader C. J. Mahaney," *Relevant* magazine, February 15, 2019
- "Abuse of Faith: 20 Years, 700 Victims: Southern Baptist Sexual Abuse Spreads as Leaders Resist Reforms," *The Houston Chronicle*, February 10, 2019.
- "The Crusading Bloggers Exposing Sexual Assault in Protestant Churches," *The Washington Post*, June 3, 2019
- "Her Evangelical Megachurch Was Her Hold. Then Her Daughter Said She Was Molested by a Minister," *The New York Times*, June 10, 2019

Contemporary evangelicalism's witness has suffered another new low by its affair with Donald Trump's presidency.[10] American historian Kristin Du Mez sees it as "the culmination of evangelicals' embrace of militant masculinity, an ideology that enshrines patriarchal authority and condones the callous display of power, at home and abroad."[11] How do church leaders that bear the name of Jesus Christ tolerate something contrary to the proclamations of Christianity? Why has the church morphed into an opposite enterprise, a Babel of public scandal and confusion?

As the title of this book suggests, I use an oxymoronic phrase "Babel church" to depict a kind of Christianity that not only generates unethical misconduct but alienates people from God and from a true sense of reality. By "Babel church," I refer to models of Christian ministry that first create a public and sensational impression, but later, often times, instead of reflecting the self-denial and humility of Christ, resemble the tower of Babel, a project of gigantic proportions, of ambition and of ungodliness.

Babel churches can be identified by some common organizational characteristics. First, leaders of Babel churches are religious entrepreneurs who utilize innovative techniques (technology, communication and organizational methods) in order to attract a following. And their charismatic leadership often has a narcissistic, self-serving component. Second, these entrepreneurial leaders generally use persuasive rhetoric and invoke the

---

10. See Galli, "Trump Should Be Removed." In recent years, there has been much discussion on this topic, which will deserve a separate elaboration. See Denker, *Red State Christians*; Stewart, *Power Worshippers*; Du Mez, *Jesus and John Wayne*; Posner, *Unholy*; Sider, *Spiritual Danger of Donald Trump*.

11. Du Mez, *Jesus and John Wayne*, 3.

manifest destiny of their ministries to legitimize the cause and to mobilize the masses. They and their church projects are keen about "making a name" for themselves by using media and technology. Third, the visible success of these Babel churches often leads to a social trend of mimicry by other church ministries, giving rise to some socially-engineered movements that potentially breed a corporate narcissism. Fourth, and most ironically, within the course of their ambitious expansions, Babel churches' attempt to maintain a positive public image often fails by way of scandalous exposé by the same media publicity. Just as the scandal of Babel was preceded by a spiritual movement fueled by innovation and publicity, what precedes these contemporary fallouts are often once-popular "movements" of the evangelical world that enjoyed an immense media spotlight. Unfortunately, these patterns have been recurring phenomena among evangelical movements in America for more than a generation.

The Rise and Fall of Evangelical Movements

For a very long time, evangelicals have belonged to a restless crowd, eager to see what the next big movement will be. They do so as if only something of a gigantic size proves that the Spirit of God is indeed at work in this world. Some entrepreneurial leaders even ventured to manufacture certain artificial movements of this sort. Since the wide use of mass media techniques in the 1970s, American evangelicalism has produced one movement after another. Some lasted for a decade or two; others only a few years. It would be fair to say that the trendiness of American evangelicalism has kept pace with greater social trendiness as coached by media and technology.[12] Indeed, many have come to the faith and experienced genuine changes in their walk with God. But in the public square, unfortunately, these movements left Christianity with less credibility in the eyes of the public.

Due to the length of this book and for the sake of argument, I do not intend to review all these evangelical movements but have chosen to present a selective survey of some movements that share certain alarming patterns—a fast rise to fame and then a subsequent fall from grace, damaging the credibility of evangelical Christianity. In all these cases, mass media contributed to both the rise and fall of the movement.

12. I thank Michael Barbalas for an insightful contribution on this point.

BABEL CHURCH

Televangelism (1970s–1980s)

Since the spread of television as a mass communication tool in the 1960s, a group of religious entrepreneurs integrated their ministry with television broadcasts. By the late 1980s, televangelism became "the most characteristic and remunerative expression of American religion."[13] Its innovative approach upgraded American evangelicalism to a new level. However, soon afterwards, televangelists who had achieved the fame and popularity of movie stars, such as Pentecostal preacher Oral Roberts, PTL Club host and Heritage USA founder Jim Bakker, and founder of SonLife Broadcasting Network Jimmy Swaggart, were each mired in financial and sexual scandals.

Megachurches or Seeker Churches (1990s–2000s)

Shortly after the rise and fall of televangelists around the 1980s, American society saw the emergence of megachurches.[14] By the 1990s, while most Protestant denominations had plateaued in membership, megachurches emerged and grew by offering new religious experiences. The innovative element in this trend was anti-traditionalism by way of fresh and changing rituals of worship. When leaders of these ministries appeared on the scene, they claimed to be making history. These megachurches have been characterized by high-profile publicity through an impressive line-up of publishing houses, media enterprises, associations, and conferences, in an effort to maintain their influence. The buzz words included "high-impact," "fast growth," "experiential," and "movement." Some megachurch campuses became Christian tourist destinations for those who desired to replicate their success.

American historian Martin Marty has famously and critically said that "Megachurch is . . . an invention of the Age of Greed."[15] His prophetic call became an enduring reality for the next two decades. Many key figures in this trend, such as New Life Church founder Ted Haggard, Calvary Chapel pastor Chuck Smith, and Harvest Bible Church pastor James MacDonald, were later found to have engaged in sexual or financial

---

13. Schultze, *Televangelism and American Culture*, 11.

14. A megachurch is usually defined as a Protestant congregation with more than 2,000 worshippers attending weekly services. See Thumma and Travis, *Beyond Megachurch Myths*. Elisha, *Moral Ambition*, 3.

15. Marty, "Minichurch and Megachurch."

8

misconduct. The fall of Willow Creek Community Church pastor Bill Hybels during the middle of the #MeToo movement, given Hybels's titanic influence during a few decades, has caused collateral damage to the overall credibility of American evangelicalism.

Promise Keepers (1990s–2000s)

Promise Keepers (PK) began as a ministry promoting conservative family values for Christian men. It held large rallies in football stadiums and drew tens of thousands of men within a few years of its founding. By 1997, the movement had expanded to eighteen cities. It had a rally at the National Mall in Washington, DC, attracting around one million men. But months after this culminating march, the movement too began to show signs of decline, mainly due to financial difficulties. After a failed attempt to boost media visibility through a millennial march in 2000, the movement lost its newsworthiness and faded. Not scandalous as the other movements listed here, probably given the narrow niche it had, Promise Keepers represents many masculinity projects on a smaller scale, such as the Purity Culture. It also shows common "Babel church" patterns that are worth analyzing in this volume.

Young, Restless, and Reformed (2000s–2010s)

If televangelism and megachurches were two trends that incorporated the superficiality and sensationalism of show business into faith and worship, in a decade or so, the pendulum had swung to another side of intellectualism and Reformation orthodoxy. A new movement known as Young, Restless, and Reformed (or YRR) emerged. In 2008, Colin Hansen, an editor of *Christianity Today*, wrote a book that gave the movement its name.[16] In 2009, the "movement" also caught the attention of *Time* magazine, which ranked the emerging New Calvinism among young American evangelicals as one of the "Ten Ideas Changing the World Right Now."[17] Its growing influence also promoted masculine Christianity to a higher level. As an effect, the evangelical mainstream saw a "growing popularity of 'biblical patriarchy.'"[18] But by 2019, some stars of this movement,

16. Hansen, *Young, Restless, Reformed*, 107.
17. Van Biema, "New Calvinism."
18. Du Mez, *Jesus and John Wayne*, 203.

such as co-founder of Mars Hill Church Mark Driscoll, Covenant Life Church pastor Joshua Harris, and founder of Sovereign Grace Ministries C.J. Mahaney, have gained notoriety, and have either been exposed by the #MeToo movement or cited for abuse of power.

To sum up, at their start-up phases, the trend-setters of the above movements wanted visible successes that would gain media publicity. This was often achieved by using some new technique in doing church. Embedded in American's relentless consumerism and celebrity culture, the Babel church model churned out celebrity pastors whose personal charisma often attracted a following. Like the surrounding culture, they identified success with size, media visibility, and status. Their followers also shared a central belief about how to do church in today's world—the bigger, the better; the more well-known, the better. They termed it as "Christian influence" returning to the public square. But here is exactly the irony and inevitable subversion—the power and reputational capital granted by media soon created its own abuse, subsequent cover-ups, and eventually the fallout. The same mass media that elevated them to celebrity status later hungered for newsworthy scandals within these churches.

When some ministry empires expanded overseas, this Babel church model of fast fame and fallout repeated itself in other lands. Globally, churches that are supposed to lift up the name of Jesus Christ have become Babel towers of fame, ambition, and manipulation. This book is an analytical reflection on how certain forms of Christianity, in our age of globalization, urbanization, and the spread of mass media technology, became the antithesis of what they are supposed to be.

Babel: From Public Fame to Public Scandal

The main biblical passage that informs this writing project is found in Genesis 11:1–9. I refer to the biblical narrative of Babel as a hermeneutical framework for exploring the structural causes of ethical failures among evangelical leaders. Although my exegetical exercise centers around the passage about Babel, in sociological analysis as well as cultural exegesis, I also draw from real-life examples where churches demonstrate signs of manipulated falsehoods and unreality. Materials such as media coverage, ministry websites, book publications, and other public records provide ample data for me. Within this volume I also reference classical social theories as well as contemporary research publications that help illuminate

INTRODUCTION

the deeper causes. This current study intersects with other works of evangelical ethics that discuss contemporary phenomena in certain types of churches, such as televangelism, the megachurch movement, or other examples of American evangelicalism. It also engages with the ethical evaluation of their import and ramifications overseas.

Babel as Biblical Narrative and Cultural Metaphor

The story of Babel took place after the flood receded and human beings gained another chance to flourish on earth. Despite God's promise not to wipe out humanity with another flood, humans felt anxious about what was to come. They wanted to find new strength by creating something tangible, something bigger than themselves. Genesis 11:1–9 uses 121 words to depict such a project. The details about these builders' actions and speech are full of excitement, single-mindedness, and determination. Some scholars consider this passage the climax of the pre-patriarchal narrative.[19]

The early chapters of Genesis show that the human race, as God's created beings, also participated in the co-creation of the world. In this process, they experienced three major crises with regard to their relationship with God and each other. The first was a result of their disobedience in Eden. The second crisis preceded the great flood of Noah's time. The third crisis was Babel.[20] A theological theme arises repeatedly—even bearing God's image, human beings could not resolve a fundamental problem: their knowledge could not help to restore the world to a peaceful balance. Rather, their actions led to continued confusion and alienation. Such is the picture of human spiritual history, as German political philosopher Eric Voegelin comments.

> [Mankind] . . . has difficulties in finding the right balance of his existence and is over-bearingly inclined to reach out toward the divinity of which he is only an image. He is thrown back to an understanding of his condition by the consciousness of death, of his human passing compared with divine lasting; he is made aware of the precariousness and weakness of his existence by overpowering natural catastrophes . . .[21]

---

19. Leder, "City and Altar Building."
20. Voegelin, *Order and History*, 55–56.
21. Voegelin, *Order and History*, 56.

From the beginning, Babel's builders did not consult or consider God; human will prevailed. Church Fathers such as John Chrysostom and Augustine proposed that Babel might have been a project initiated by Nimrod, who was proud, ambitious, and despised God's authority.[22] This may explain the willful leadership that left an imprint on the whole enterprise.

Moreover, the builders of Babel were driven by the self-aggrandizing desire "to make a name" for themselves. Behind this strong purpose was the fear that they might be scattered. Babel-builders designed this city-with-a-tower project to be reaching to the heavens. It was literally a skyscraper acting as a cosmic centerpiece in the post-flood world, to demonstrate the collective might of the one human race. Nevertheless, in the end, contrary to their hope, this group of ambitious yet frustrated builders were identified in history as an epitome of God's action by bringing disorder and confusion.

> The narrative is as symmetrically structured as any since chapter 1 of Genesis. Its beginning with "whole earth" and "one language" (v.1) is nicely balanced in verse 9 with "all the earth" and "the language of all the earth." These verses form an envelope for the narrative.... The structure ... shows that the resolve of humankind is in conflict with the resolve of God. The action of Yahweh responds to and correlates deliberately with the actions of humanity though the two parts are presented as sin and judgment.[23]

The biblical narrative of Babel has become a powerful cultural metaphor to mean division, disconcert, and confusion. Based on these distinct features, the Babel narrative continues to serve as a symbol for how human pride and ambition turn out. One of the end products is tribalism. As biblical scholar Walter Brueggemann writes, it is a "self-made unity" by which humanity forms a "fortress mentality." He continues: "This unity attempts to establish a cultural, human oneness without reference to the threats, promises, or mandates of God. It seeks to construct a world free of the danger of the holy and immune from the terrors of God in history. It is a unity grounded in fear and characterized by coercion."[24]

Many trace the origins of human linguistic plurality and resultant unfortunate challenges in global communication to the story of Babel. Some also refer to it as the origins of globalization, more specifically global urbanism,

22. Louth et al., *Ancient Christian Commentary*, 166–70.
23. Brueggemann, *Genesis*, 98.
24. Brueggemann, *Genesis*, 100.

which involves the transformation of human living spaces into commodities and symbols of self-identity that often are associated with glamor and importance. Thus social and material progress is identified with the height of skyscrapers. Nations and cities of the world rush to compete by building the next architectural spectacle. In 2015, *The Economist* reports a "skyscraper boom," listing more buildings over 200 meters tall around the globe than in past eras.[25] Even social analysts today know that architectural projects like these do something to people's collective consciousness.

Human beings can design and create their built environment, but the latter also takes on a life of its own in influencing the inhabitants. Self-importance tends to make human beings lose the right perspective. This distortion of perspective with regard to the purpose of life tends to breed dissonance and conflicts that infest all realms of modern life. As Old Testament scholar Gerhard von Rad points out, "this evolution and slow rise to cultural greatness is accompanied by an ever-growing estrangement of man from God that was bound to lead to a catastrophe."[26] For example, with economic neoliberalism, the world is becoming flat. The global economy and a competitive urban lifestyle serve as one manifestation of such flatness, which has affected more and more cultures and societies, so that ambition, fame, and achievement are valued as the normative goals in life. But this flatness has exacerbated moral irresponsibility, divisions, and conflicts.

Babel was also a media project through architectural signaling with its height and gigantic size. Today, mass media, which has spread hand in hand with the trend of global urbanism, has played a crucial role in shaping how people perceive reality, both near and far. The role of the one voice that shouted "Let us . . . make a name for ourselves" in Genesis 11 has been amplified by the all-encompassing bombardments of mass media, the main venue today for name-making among fellow human beings. Politicians, economists, engineers, business people, and religious groups all find mass media to be a means of strategic influence, because media shape the consciousness of the public. What Canadian philosopher Marshall McLuhan criticized about advertising and mass media entertainment is also applicable today: "Ours is the first age in which many thousands of the best-trained individual minds have made it a full-time business to get inside the collective public mind . . . in order to manipulate, exploit, control . . ."[27]

25. "Towers of Babel."
26. Von Rad, *Old Testament Theology*, 160.
27. McLuhan, *Mechanical Bride*, v.

Without this undergirding system of meaning in place, the physical global structures exist like a body without a soul. Compared to the physical, built environment people live in, this mental or spiritual realm is an arena for competing meaning systems, a contest among invisible but powerful Babel projects in the contemporary world.

Babel as Religious Entrepreneurism

The builders of Babel were religious entrepreneurs who attempted to cross the heaven-earth divide.[28] Then and now, the builders are inevitably driven by the desire for power, the ambition for wider influence, and the will to achieve. The psychological gains from getting projects accomplished can become addictive to them. Such entrepreneurial efforts are often strengthened by leaders who demonstrate a certain personal charisma. They exert great persuasive power in communication. Because they are good at laying out exciting mental maps for people, such charismatic and entrepreneurial leaders tend to attract large crowds of followers.

Entrepreneurial leadership and persuasion are key to the Babel narrative. "Making a name" and "reaching heaven" mobilized a mass workforce that embraced the purpose of building so as not to be scattered. Scripture does not tell us how long they worked on the project before God intervened, but it likely was an expansive project that involved more people than any previous enterprise. In some ways, even Noah's building of the ark could not compare to the commotion this Babel project brought to humanity. Interestingly, though, here is a paradoxical contrast between the ark and Babel: when God initiated a project, such as Noah's ark, few people followed; but when human beings came up with an idea to reach the heaven by their own design, the following swelled.

With the entertainment industry becoming the focal point of contemporary American society, more and more churches began to operate like brand-name enterprises, offering celebrity pastors for members to follow. Usually, a marketing team around this pastor streamlines content for maximum reach and prepares crisis management when scandals follow. They operate on Babel mode, relying on human strength in managing and maneuvering. As Pope Benedict XVI, in a Pentecost homily, said,

---

28. Hoselitz, "Early History of Entrepreneurial Theory." Swedberg, "Social Science View."

INTRODUCTION

[W]hat is Babel? It is . . . a kingdom in which people have concentrated so much power they think they no longer need depend on a God who is far away. They believe they are so powerful they can build their own way to heaven in order to open the gates and put themselves in God's place . . . We don't realize we are reliving the same experience as Babel.[29]

During the past century, the history of Christian mission had shifting geographical centers, from Europe to America, and then to Asia, Latin America, and Africa. With global economic liberalization and human migration, Christian mission has decentralized into an era of "everyone reaching out to everyone else." Today churches in South Korea, China, and African nations are sending missionaries to other regions of the world. Having no particular center of missional work means that the Spirit of God is seen to be at work everywhere. And this is certainly true. But it also means that a Babel-type "movement" can also happen anywhere. Americans often even expect to see the next movement happening in a foreign land, especially one experiencing poverty and oppression.

Some Marxist scholars might offer an insightful observation here. In a global consumer society, churches are embedded in the commercial structures that intensify human beings' alienation with the progression of capitalism. All people and things have become commodities, generating an endless lineup of false consciousness, conspicuous consumption, and self-alienation, which all eventually turn into fetishism.[30] Interpersonal relationships that should be founded on trust and love have unfortunately been turned into commodities in market transactions.[31] Global, missional entrepreneurism may have subverted the essence of Christianity on an even larger scale.

Contemporary Babel Churches

The contemporary Babel church is a reflection of many social, cultural, and economic currents in our social psychology and public life. It thrives at the intersection between a consumeristic macro-culture and a narcissistic subculture. Such ministries usually have an insatiable thirst for

29. "Unity Can Only Exist."
30. See Bloch, *Atheism in Christianity*, 251–57.
31. On modern fetishism and late capitalism and their symbols, see Žižek, *Plague of Fantasies*, 86–126.

expansion. They are led by public Christian personalities who often later reveal alienated lives. Power, control, and impression management characterize these Babel churches.

Rather than confining the objects of analysis to one particular movement, I hope to look into some deeper and broader factors in today's evangelical cultural landscape. It is not my intention to classify certain movements or types of churches as Babel churches, although certain "movements" are more susceptible than others to the spiritual diseases mentioned here. The analysis is also not limited to American evangelicalism, for the Babel model of Christianity has already been exported overseas through missional entrepreneurism, global urbanism, neoliberal economics, and consumerism.

Methodologically, this book adopts a socio-theological-ethical approach by attending to social structural and cultural factors that help shape churches' organizational behavior. I find it necessary to engage with thoughtful scholars across different disciplines, such as social theory, philosophy, theology, and ethics. I also examine the biblical basis, sociological processes, and ethical ramifications of this phenomenon to present a richer understanding.

What This Book Is (and Isn't) About

This book is about how the scandal of Babel continues to plague the church today, when globalization has incorporated all of us into one synchronized community. It is an analytical diagnosis of the pathological symptoms that recur in today's media-savvy evangelical world. The realization that being a witness for Jesus Christ in the world requires Christians to be self-critical and discerning has motivated the writing of this book.

When it comes to why and when Christianity becomes a source of alienation for the person and the culture, an unthinking believer might say "There are certainly wheat and tares growing together." Or alternatively, "It's all the devil's work!" is declared to cap off the conversation. Here and now, I would point us to a famous Western idiom: "The Devil is in the details"—it takes day-to-day form in our rhetorical hyperboles, self-promoting use of mass media, ambitious exaggerations in global mission, and impression management during image-threatening crises.

While many books have sought to offer theological advice on the crisis of evangelical leadership, few have presented clear, systematic analysis that

INTRODUCTION

allows readers to reflect deeply on how the characteristics of evangelical entrepreneurism correlate with existing structures and trends in mass media and globalization. For example, *Forbes*'s ranking of richest pastors in 2019 reveals that over half of these celebrity preachers are outside of the United States, but each of them established a media empire, often through television or megachurch networks, that resonates with some passing trends in America. Do such rankings and other news of evangelical scandals around the globe provide us more than mere statistics and facts? This book attempts to offer a more wholistic understanding. It points out the sources of spiritual temptation that might be amplified in these spheres where churches are at high risk of leadership failures. I believe examination of similar failures in the church may reveal enduring themes. They might teach us about how sinful human nature is expressed through church leadership, and why we fail to maintain the church's credibility in relating to society and culture. Thus I affirm the need for structural analysis because organizational behavior tends to follow a somewhat predictable pattern.

The analytical approach of this book is new on several fronts. First, the social processes behind leadership failures in the church have until now received only scant scholarly attention. This is even more true after the #MeToo movement. Many recently published books discuss these same phenomena from only an observational perspective. Very few public theologians have been able to incorporate this important societal development into their theologizing.[32] Second, there has been a lack of an interdisciplinary approach among scholars who pay attention to the dynamics of power in an evangelical context. Thus, I endeavor to engage with social theorists, philosophers, communication experts, and religious scholars. Third, unsatisfied with an ethnocentric approach that deals with only American evangelicalism, I include an analysis of the same phenomena from global churches. Fourth, this book makes a distinctive contribution by putting three large pieces of the puzzle together: evangelicalism, mass media, and globalization. This book seeks to contribute to this cross-sphere understanding. As evangelical author Andrew Byers writes, the church needs "a hermeneutical project in the church's wider efforts of trying to understand the technological mediascape of the 21st century."[33]

This book is about failures in America's evangelical churches and their social and global implications. I use some examples from the cultural

32. One scholarly contribution is Reaves, "#MeToo Jesus."
33. Byers, *TheoMedia*, 14.

scene of American evangelicalism because it has been the upstream influence. Concerning the "McDonaldization" phenomenon of global churches, America offered the archetype for such a chain store model. Also, since America boasts a free media where many leadership failures were exposed to the public, these case studies are the best documented public data. That being said, this book does not seek to offer a representative survey or overview. Even when referring to certain specific movements, such as megachurches, I do not claim in a wholesale manner that all megachurches are Babel churches. I reckon that, even across these movements, there is a great diversity in terms of their origins, development, and future trajectories. I seek to avoid over-generalizations while still pointing out some recurring patterns that are often ignored by observers.

This book is also about deception in the church and how we often fail to detect spiritual temptations for what they are. From the #MeToo and #ChurchToo movements, we see recurring patterns where victims and advocates experienced pushbacks, ostracism, and even denigration from their own church communities. The reality is that Christians often do not recognize evil for what it is. Although it is our common prayer that God may deliver us from the evil one, what if we take evil for good and good for evil? If so, who is there to then stop us from being tempted?

As a response, I offer an analysis of evangelical ethics that involves a careful reading of its mediated and globalized contexts. I map out and provide readers with a framework for identifying a critical theology of evangelical movements that relates to today's world, a world saturated by mass media where spiritual temptations take familiar, everyday forms—sometimes perhaps too familiar and mundane to be taken seriously. But once these desires come to fruition, the results can be devastating for the public witness of the church. The book seeks to challenge this everyday complicity and recognizes these structural or social sins for what they are. As contemporary American theologian Jennifer McBride analyzes,

> Our everyday living makes us complicit in sin as members of a common humanity, and such sin and injustice are too pervasive for us to extricate ourselves entirely from, in part because of the structural and intergenerational nature of sin and in part because of the tightly interwoven character of all aspects of human life. Economic, environmental, agricultural, technological, racial, class, national, and international sin and injustice form a tight web within which we live and move and have our being, and in a

INTRODUCTION

powerful or affluent society, our lives effortlessly benefit in countless, unrecognized ways from some or all of these structures.[34]

This book is also a reflection on the problematic media environment created by media professionals who are largely ignorant of (or sometimes even indifferent to) how the work they deem so valuable for increasing freedom and democracy has hurt local communities. I do not offer a wholesale criticism against mass media and communication technologies; rather, I affirm their importance. In fact, I consider them so important that we cannot afford to be uncritical. In other words, I am not concerned about whether the church should make use of mass media but *how* the church should engage with mass media. I also reckon that evangelicals, coming from a diverse background with regard to age cohorts, gender, cultural, and political backgrounds, hold a variety of views and approaches about the use of mass media.[35]

I find it necessary to state from the beginning that my position toward the forces of mass media and globalization is neither lighthearted optimism nor apocalyptic pessimism but one of critical engagement. It is exactly because we now live such in a fragmented world that mass media wields considerable power to shape our perception. We need to treat media as social institutions that also function in a power sphere, just as evangelical churches do. With power comes accountability. It is our duty to not misuse that power.

As a female scholar, I also write this book in the aftermath of the #MeToo and #ChurchToo movements as a reflection on the reason women's voices need to be heard in evangelical circles. French sociologist-theologian Jacques Ellul analyzes the relationship between the subversion of Christianity and the marginalization of women.

> [W]hen Christianity became a power or authority, this worked against women. A strange perversion, yet fully understandable when we allow that women represent precisely the most innovative elements in Christianity: grace, love, charity, a concern for living creatures, nonviolence, an interest in little things, the hope of new beginnings—the very elements that Christianity was setting aside in favor of glory and success.[36]

34. McBride, *Church for the World*, 141.
35. See Smith, *American Evangelicalism*; Clark, *From Angels to Aliens*; Schultz, *Christianity and the Mass Media*.
36. Ellul, *Subversion of Christianity*, 33–34.

Lastly, this book does not attempt to offer a simple solution to evangelical leadership failure. In fact, if anything else, this book advocates against the quick-fix mentality when it comes to how to do church ministry. That mindset has been part of the problem, as I will show. Many ethical principles are implied in the ongoing analysis. The only certain antidote to this systemic disease, as I discuss at the end of this book, is in Philippians 2:1–11. In the conclusion of this book I reflect on the relevance of this text to the main themes of my reflection.

The main body of this book has six chapters. Chapter 2, "Technique and Entrepreneurism," discusses the defining role of technique and entrepreneurial leadership in shaping the entire Babel project from its beginning. Chapter 3, "Media and Reputational Capital," analyzes the sociological production of fame for the church in today's mass media environment. Evangelical entrepreneurs are like fish in water when using consumerist trends from the wider popular culture. They create celebrity pastors whose influence potentially shapes a faith community into a narcissistic subculture. Chapter 4, "Engineering a Movement," engages the question of how a broader movement is brought into place with the help of religious media, technology, and consumerism. Here the evangelical world intersects with mass media professionalism to produce an entangled, hate-love relationship between the two. Chapter 5, "Scandalous Confusion," discusses the collapse of Babel projects by way of God's intervention through truth-telling from a broken community. Chapter 6, "Global Epidemic," explores the global phase of a Babel Christian culture when global urbanism and impersonalism further exacerbate the problem. In the final chapter, I offer a reflection on leadership ethics by drawing on Philippians 2, a christological hymn of Jesus Christ's self-denial and humility. Here I also engage with the evangelical crisis during the #MeToo movement from a public theological perspective. These reflections may serve as a catalyst for future conversations.

This book is intended for scholars, church leaders, and observers who are troubled by contemporary ecclesial trends that have been shaped and even subverted by an uncritical embrace of effective techniques to expand Christian "influence." It offers an analytical read about the collective pathological behavior of contemporary evangelicalism. Strategy and communication specialists in churches and Christian organizations might also benefit from these discussions. Because this book often quotes scholarly publications, it might be a heavy read for the general public. Students

INTRODUCTION

of sociology and theology are likely to be interested in an interdisciplinary approach of this book. It is also intended for scholars and thoughtful readers who ponder how the crisis of modernity relates to the church in everyday forms.[37] I also hope that this book can be read by leaders of the global church, especially budding Protestant communities that are influenced by the downstream effect of American evangelicalism. Churches around the world face these same challenges.

---

37. By "modernity" I refer to the historical development of market capitalism, rationalization, urbanization, and technological progress. While many scholars prefer to use "postmodernism" when describing our time, I use "late modernity" in this book. I will expand on this in the last chapter. See Giddens, *Consequences of Modernity*; Voegelin, *Modernity without Restraint*.

Chapter 2

Technique and Entrepreneurism

> Now the whole world had one language and a common speech. As people moved eastward, they found a plain in Shinar and settled there. They said to each other, "Come, let's make bricks and bake them thoroughly." They used brick instead of stone, and tar for mortar. —Genesis 11:1–2

The Babel narrative is a short but exemplary piece of Hebrew storytelling. Among its many compositional techniques are word play, chiasmus, paronomasia, and alliteration that together unify and accentuate the dramatic tale. According to Scripture, after people settled in the plain of Shinar, an activistic and enterprising voice declared: "Come, let us make bricks." Scripture does not inform us of specific names, but we can infer that the command came from a few people who had assumed leadership. Not content with the old nomadic life, they searched for a certain fulfillment and aspiration.

These leaders were also entrepreneurial innovators. First, they identified a new building technique, possibly used by people in the area. Second, they applied an organizational logic for mobilizing the masses. The command in Genesis 11:2 delivered an urgency and clear specifications for action. Immediately, the people got behind the effort. Nobody questioned and everybody contributed their labor.

Genesis 11:1–4 already shows certain key ingredients of religious entrepreneurism in the time of Babel. The word "entrepreneur" often means someone with the ability to get things done in service of a new productive goal.[1]

---

1. Hoselitz, "Early History of Entrepreneurial Theory"; Swedberg, "Social Science View."

Entrepreneurial behaviors range from the innovation of a new technique to the discovery of a new niche market and the creation of new institutions. German sociologist Max Weber's theory of entrepreneurship highlights that as charismatic leaders endowed with persuasive power in communication capacity, entrepreneurs are able to attract large followings. They are also good at delivering a broader vision and at impressing it on others.[2] To Austrian economist Joseph Schumpeter, entrepreneurs play a crucial role in using new inventions and innovative techniques to produce new products and modes of production. Through incessantly revolutionizing economic innovation, entrepreneurs often need to subvert old organizational models. Schumpeter refers to this mutation process as "creative destruction."[3] When applying these aspects of entrepreneurship to the religious realm, it takes on another propelling dimension—its visible success may lead to the claim of divine appointment, a form of spiritual and moral capital.

Ingredients of Babel Entrepreneurism

Innovative Techniques: ". . . brick instead of stone"

According to French theologian and sociologist Jacques Ellul, "technique" refers to any "operation carried out in accordance with a certain method in order to attain a particular goal."[4] It includes any standardized means to attain a predetermined result. As the story of Babel progresses, we see that the people adopted a new building technique ("brick instead of stone"). Swiss theologian Karl Barth considers this use of new technique neutral: "This does not necessarily mean that it regards itself as capable of shaping its own future and destiny and becoming its own lord. It does not necessarily entail a repetition of the sin of Adam, Cain and the whole of the first humanity which perished in the flood." Barth, nonetheless, also comments that the problem lies in "this step towards civilization, this augmentation of man's creative capacity in relation to himself and nature and his fellows."[5]

The leadership desired a certain organizational principle to make Babel into an edifice of concentrated power that dominated the landscape of humanity. Its urbanism with monumental architecture would

---

2. Weber, *Theory of Social and Economic Organization*.
3. Schumpeter, *Capitalism, Socialism and Democracy*, 81–86.
4. Ellul, *Technological Society*, 19.
5. Barth, *Church Dogmatics*, 314.

serve social, ceremonial, and bureaucratic purposes. Complementary to this cosmic center were system and hierarchy, formal rules and informal norms, centralized techniques and promotion of legitimacy. As human experience shows, generally "with the aid of technology, spiritual needs are becoming more rationalized, monitored, and more directly accessible, thereby fundamentally altering relations between religious producers and religious consumers."[6]

Unfortunately, technological innovations at Babel projects would soon become a machinery of coercion, with those at the very top of its hierarchy imposing demands on those at the bottom. As Jewish scholar Shai Held comments, the Babel story is about a "coercive uniformity" at the expense of individualism and creativity.[7]

Manifest Destiny: "Reaching the Heavens"

After the brick-making technique was tested and found workable, the leadership began to mobilize more people to join the project. By broadcasting the goal to reach the heavens, Babel leadership delivered a powerful rhetoric of persuasion. This new skyscraper promises to bring humanity into contact with the divine. Some commentators also point out that the use of a ziggurat to reach to the heavens is part of a Babylonian theology, for "their mutual exhortation 'let us build for ourselves' contain those letters *n, b,* and *l*" which implicitly refer to the main temple in Babylon, meaning "the house with the raised head."[8] Based on these details, Genesis views this ancient skyscraper as "another human effort to become like God and have intercourse with him."[9] Other scholars debate the symbolism as implying earthly blessing or fertility.[10]

The book of Genesis makes a marked contrast between altar-building and city construction. Before Abram, people built cities without seeing divine appearances. The patriarchs began a different pattern by building altars only at the locations where God appeared and spoke to them. The initiation of the Babel project reverts that pattern and forms an immediate contrast to Noah's previous altar-building activity. Old Testament scholar

6. Roof, *Spiritual Marketplace*, 103.
7. Held, "Babel Story."
8. Wenham, *Genesis 1–15*, 239.
9. Wenham, *Genesis 1–15*, 239.
10. Keel, *Symbolism of the Biblical World*, 116–18.

Arie Leder points out that it was "an undesirable means of connecting earth to heaven for heaven's blessings."[11] This comment is consistent with Karl Barth's summation—the real problem lies with "the fact that this one people wants to make for itself a city as an instrument and guarantee, invented and fashioned by itself, of the unity resolved and to be maintained by it, . . . but in its own right and in an attempted equality with Him [God] on the basis of its own work."[12]

The rhetoric of manifest destiny intensifies the charisma of Babel leadership, which then translates into a new form of authority. Max Weber gives a classical definition of such charismatic authority: "[charisma is] . . . a certain quality of an individual personality by virtue of which he is considered extraordinary and treated as endowed with supernatural, superhuman, or at least specifically exceptional powers or qualities."[13] As much as human societies gravitate towards charismatic leadership, it may often lead to ethical challenges. According to Old Testament scholar Walter Brueggemann, resorting to a divine purpose veils the pursuit of conformity that may prove to be oppressive.

> It may not need to be presumed that the Babel proposition is an anti-religious proposal, for religion can provide exactly that kind of unity and certify social oppression. In such a world, the tower can participate in religiosity as a symbol of unity . . . to establish conformities or to construct a "sacred canopy" which consolidates human freedom.[14]

Babel entrepreneurs delivered a triumphalist statement, communicating their authority on matters of humanity's spiritual destiny. Expressing no recognition of their own limits, they became complicit in the pride, exploitation, and glorification of power.

Mass Mobilization: "Come, Let us . . ."

After having developed the techniques and declaring a divine purpose, Babel entrepreneurs wanted to engineer a mass religious movement. They needed the participation of many followers. As social scientists point out,

11. Leder, "City and Altar Building."
12. Barth, *Church Dogmatics*, 314.
13. Weber, *Economy and Society*, 241.
14. Brueggemann, *Genesis*, 100.

the forming of charismatic authority is a two-way street between charismatic leaders and their followers—"Like beauty, charisma is in the eye of the beholder."[15] Max Weber's emphasis on the social orientation of this concept highlights that charisma is often attributed to a leader by his or her followers. Contemporary research also affirms this aspect of mutual reinforcement.[16] "Leaders are not charismatic unless their followers attribute charisma to them."[17] To a large extent, this attribution occurs because charismatic leaders offer emotive gifts that satisfy their audience: "Once someone has been ascribed with charismatic power, disciples seek an affirmation for what they feel, and feel gratified when they find it."[18] Furthermore,

> The leader relies on the adoration and respect of his followers; the follower is attracted to the omnipotence and charisma of the leader. The leader uses polarizing rhetoric that identifies an outside enemy, bringing together leader and followers on a grandiose mission. The followers feed off the leader's certainty in order to fill their own empty senses of self. Interestingly, in this mutually reinforcing relationship, both are prone to a form of narcissism.[19]

Canadian sociologist of religion Lorne Dawson theorizes regarding the precariousness of charismatic leadership:

> As Weber classically presented them, charismatic leaders are romantic disrupters who abrogate and transcend social conventions. They tend to break the existing patterns of authority or harness even older ones to new circumstances. . . . At the same time, they impose new demands for obedience and new standards of service and sacrifice, but they do so within an emotionally charged framework of relationships and activities. . . . Claims to charismatic authority by a leader and their followers can bring persecution from outside the group and lead to power struggles within the group, and both processes tend to aggravate the tyranny and instability further.[20]

---

15. Riis and Woodhead, *Sociology of Religious Emotion*, 164. Post, "Narcissism and the Charismatic."

16. Immergut and Kosut, "Visualising Charisma"; Wignall, "Man after God's Own Heart."

17. Corcoran and Wellman, "'People Forget He's Human.'"

18. Riis and Woodhead, *Sociology of Religious Emotions*, 165.

19. DeGroat, *When Narcissism Comes to Church*, 23.

20. Dawson, *Comprehending Cults*, 154.

Babel entrepreneurs also ushered in a logic for solidarity that was based on anxiety and fear. In fact, as Karl Barth comments, they minimized the blessing of unity through a common speech but magnified a fear for the future. Such fear-mongering prepared the social psychological foundation for this Babel enterprise. Barth adds:

> What is wrong is the anxiety underlying this construction, the forgetting of the name and unity already enjoyed, and the resultant arrogance of thinking that man himself can and must take himself as he takes brick and mortar, and make himself the lord of his history, constituting the work of providence his own work. . . . [I]t is obviously a departure from grace. . . . [A]s the overarching of supreme human culture by a form of supreme human religion, it is most radically and forcefully directed against God, and therefore a work which is evil in intention . . .[21]

From the start, charismatic leaders face some common legitimation problems. More often, since they are savvy in expression and rhetoric, they use these skills to shape reality and manage impressions for their followers. Thus, "the legitimacy underlying charismatic leadership must be maintained through impression management."[22] They also face the task of moderating the psychological identification of followers and of achieving new successes.

"New Ways" of Doing Church

Religious entrepreneurs in the evangelical world may fall into a few categories: visionaries, celebrity pastors, and church growth consultants. The first group of entrepreneurs are good at discovering a new technique or a niche market and fashioning a new idea to meet needs. They often term these future blueprints as "visions" from God. The second group are charismatic personalities who have certain rhetorical gifts to offer from the pulpit. They often become the "poster boy (or girl)" of a project. The last group of entrepreneurs are movement engineers who watch trends and attempt to ride waves, often using modern techniques of media communication. Together, these three groups bring about a new "brand" or movement that may attract a large following.[23]

21. Barth, *Church Dogmatics*, 314
22. Corcoran and Wellman, "'People Forget He's Human.'"
23. In evangelical circles, the term *brand* refers to a projected public image of a

Every few years, a new trend of doing church ministry becomes a fad. Usually there is something innovative about this new trend, either in its mode of communicating the message, its theological direction, or its liturgical aspect of gathering worship communities.[24] A few examples follow.

Televangelism

Since the 1970s, the invention and popularization of television has profoundly transformed American society. A few decades after religious broadcasting began via radio networks, the new medium of television fueled this industry. American journalist Carol Flake writes with a tone of sarcasm that "By the beginning of the eighties, the Lord's business had become big business." She continues:

> [E]vangelists had become entrepreneurs, and entrepreneurs had become evangelists. The phantom congregations of the nation's TV preachers had become rooted in elaborate institutions, and ordinary churches had grown into Super Churches.... [Sometimes] those services were a matter of luxury rather than necessity.[25]

For America, televangelism became the nation's own religion. It was a special Protestant hybrid cultivated in America and nurtured by the mass media, taking advantage of the cultural cues in both realms. According to American communications scholar Quentin Schultz, it has become the "flagship of American religion" and set "the style and tone of local and denominational church life," where Christians increasingly matured their faith "in the saving power of technology."[26]

Megachurches

Within the trend of megachurches, new methods include "an emphasis on contemporary music and on practical messages; featuring a wide variety

---

ministry that is essential to establish a place in the spiritual marketplace. As Bowler points out, "once shaped, it must be carefully maintained." See Bowler, *Preacher's Wife*. I thank Casey Jen for pointing me to this resource.

24. Technique is not only limited to the use of technology; it can be the rediscovery and repackaging of a much older theological resource.

25. Flake, *Redemptorama*, 49–50.

26. Schultze, *Televangelism and American Culture*, 11.

of choice in small groups and other ministries; creating an informal atmosphere; and deemphasizing denominational identity."[27] It served to fill the vacuum caused by decades of community decline as pointed out by American political scientist Robert Putnam in his classic book *Bowling Alone*. Putnam affirms that religious groups offer important social capital for American society. But he also observes that American evangelicalism has created dynamic, large groups where relationships tend to coalesce inwardly rather than towards inclusiveness for all members of society.[28]

Often, megachurches' shopping-mall-sized sanctuaries enhance a more inviting theatre experience. The pursuit of sensual, mountaintop stimulation has been adapted from the American consumer ethos, as has the stage effects of its entertainment industry. Scholars find that the appeal of modern megachurches also lies in their artistic and cultural tastes of using innovative worship styles and charismatic leadership.[29] Leaders with both spiritual charisma and outgoing personalities became stars in the pulpits. Based on a large survey of megachurch attendees, sociologists Katie E. Corcoran and James K. Wellman, Jr. find that "a charismatic bond" from both "extraordinary and ordinary qualities" serves as a primary motivation for people to join and remain at a megachurch.[30] With critical mass and ambition to achieve cultural influence, megachurches are known to offer a life system of programs tailored to members' needs.

Organizationally, megachurches tend to build quasi-denominational networks for training to expand their influence and brand loyalty. Their visible success has been accompanied by frequent rhetoric of grandiosity. In 1989, thirty-seven-year-old Bill Hybels declared, "We're on the verge of making kingdom history . . . doing things a new way for a whole new generation."[31] Rick Warren, founder of Saddleback Community Church, also elevated the demand of this niche market as "a trend all across America moving away from the small neighborhood churches to large regional-type churches."[32] Lyle Schaller, known as "the dean of church consultants" in

---

27. Sargeant, *Seeker Churches*, 7.
28. Putnam, *Bowling Alone*, 65–79.
29. Ellingson, "New Research on Megachurches"; Wellman, *Rob Bell and the New American Christianity*.
30. Corcoran and Wellman, "'People Forget He's Human.'"
31. Chandler, "Test-Marketing the Gospel."
32. Chandler, "Test-Marketing the Gospel."

America,³³ proclaimed, "The emergence of the 'megachurch' is the most important development of modern Christian history."³⁴

Promise Keepers

Promise Keepers began in 1990 with a few dozen men. The group held large rallies in football stadiums and drew tens of thousands of men over a few years. Observers affirm its timely emergence as a response to "a mass identity crisis among American males, who have for a long time felt isolated, powerless and disenfranchised by a society in transition that seems to view them as expendable."³⁵ The organization also presented itself as an effective ministry by distributing testimonials from women who say their errant husbands have been transformed into loving and godly spouses. As *The Christian Science Monitor* observes, "that awareness is moral wakefulness, and the country needs all of that it can get in the late 20th century."³⁶

This movement appeals to a niche market among evangelical males who embrace complementarian values. Its goal was to "celebrate Biblical manhood and motivate men toward a Christ-like masculinity." It repackages conservative family values with the use of sport facilities and mass marches. Scholars rank this movement as "the latest incarnation of the muscular Christianity impulse."³⁷

Young, Restless, and Reformed (YRR)

Like the Promise Keepers, YRR also appeals to a smaller niche market—evangelicals who grew discontented with watered-down theology in the broader evangelical world. Unlike the wider trends of televangelism and megachurches, YRR was a return to the root of Protestant orthodoxy and thus attracted a smaller but no less visible crowd. Based mainly on book publishing, it cultivated celebrity pastors who endorse each other and form alliance platforms or coalition conferences.

33. Neff, "CTI's Modest Dynamic Duo."
34. Schaller, "Megachurch!"
35. Andrews, "What's Wrong."
36. "Promise Keepers' Goals."
37. Balmer, *Evangelicalism in America*, 135.

YRR almost emerged as a counter-current to the both televangelism and megachurches and their theological superficiality. As a response to dissatisfaction with the evangelical *status quo*, an article in *The American Conservative* says, "Millennials are seeking old ways of doing things. This (thankfully) does not mean a return to the church of the 1950s, but it means an increasing rejection of the church of the 1990s and 2000s."[38] Theologically speaking, it resorted to something rather old. To differentiate themselves from the historical Calvinism, contemporary popularizers of Reformed theology named the trend as a "New Calvinism," and an orthodox "resurgence."[39]

In sum, the use of new techniques, organizational principles, and theologies for doing church has been central to the popularity of these aspiring religious enterprises. Technique, in a sense, sums up the "whatever-works" utilitarian ethics when attracting a crowd, either through technology, theology, or liturgy. For a time, these new models generated desirable results.

Most entrepreneurial celebrities in the American evangelical world had their own innovative breakthroughs. Billy Sunday was an early experimenter who combined Christianity and mass entertainment. Aimee Semple McPherson engineered worship space into one of the first megachurches in America. She also started her own radio station. Jim Bakker's heritage was the use of television, the Christian talk show, a satellite network, and eventually a Christian theme park. Oral Roberts, Billy Graham, and many others expanded religious broadcasting to global audiences.[40] Each innovation was a Christian version of the most popular cultural trend of its day. As religious entrepreneurs, they successfully converted mass consumer needs to a religious trend that claimed itself to be God's Spirit at work.

Here we need to make a distinction between the prosperity gospel and Babel church projects. They do share the same claims to visible success as divine blessings. But Babel church enterprises are characterized by the novelty of techniques, which not only include technological innovation but also theological repackaging. To compare the four movements, the trend of televangelism and megachurches might have overlapping arenas with prosperity gospel ministries. But the last two movements, Promise

---

38. Dreher, "Kill Your Megachurch Worship."

39. Driscoll, *Call to Resurgence*, 201.

40. Scholars disagree whether Billy Graham had his own innovation. See Bruce, *PRAY TV*, 32. Bruce asserts that Graham "has made extensive use of mass media but has done little to innovate."

Keepers and YRR, appealed to a restorationalist sentiment by putting the old wine of orthodox Protestant theology into the new wineskins of contemporary communication. They are examples of how even theology can be repackaged using new techniques.

Technique and Theology

Claiming to be helping people to meet God in their lives and to combat secularism, these entrepreneurs never considered themselves as heralds of secularism itself. But as the social critic Os Guinness says, "The two most easily recognizable hallmarks of secularization in America are the exaltation of numbers and of technique."[41] The use of technique brings efficiency, predictability, calculability and control (or at least the illusion of control), all captured by the term "McDonaldization," coined by American sociologist George Ritzer. As Scottish theologian John Drane comments, "The church's love affair with the predictability aspect of McDonaldization is a major stumbling block to effective evangelism. It can easily encourage a lack of honesty within any given congregation."[42]

Obsession with numbers and efficiency creates new anxiety, and subsequently new forms of control and outlooks on reality. "Like insecure shepherds, preachers were always counting their sheep, as well as their blessings, boasting about the size of their flocks. . . . In a zero-sum theology, one more convert for Christ and conservatism meant one less recruit for the devil and humanism."[43] Quentin J. Schultze writes that American evangelicalism's dependence on "new gadgetry" creates almost a "rhetoric of technological salvation."

> More than in other nations, Americans usually see the problem of national and worldwide evangelization in technological terms. Evangelization is normally viewed as a "mass" problem that necessitates "mass" communication. . . . Evangelicals' hope and trust in new gadgetry has often placed them at the forefront of developing and using new communications technologies. . . . American evangelicalism has produced its own rhetoric of

---

41. Guinness, *Dining with the Devil*, 49.
42. Drane, *McDonaldization of the Church*, 49.
43. Flake, *Redemptorama*, 51–52.

technological salvation. . . . [These are seen as] God's tools for worldwide evangelization.[44]

Another commonality of all these inventions lies in their intersection with American pop culture, which often creates large followings. The common devotees were more spiritually and emotionally attached to these mediated ministries than to their local church. Gradually, a kind of "brand loyalty" forms. Followers or fans of a certain brand may enthusiastically elevate it or defend its reputation. They became emotionally invested in these ministries. This phenomenon also helps to answer the question, at what point does a theology become an ideology? The answer—when it becomes entangled with tribal emotionalism and exclusivism.[45]

Many observe that such technological maneuvering often goes hand in hand with conservative theology. Schultze is also right in commenting that "today some of the most theologically conservative churches are among the leaders in religious marketing and promotion."[46] He further explains that "the strident simplicity of the conservative Protestant message makes it better suited for communication by mass media."[47] American historian Kate Blower also confirms that "megaministry was an overwhelmingly conservative Protestant phenomenon."[48] Theologically conservative groups tend to carry out such entrepreneurship because their "products" provide *certainty*. They also tend to be well-suited for the use of mass communication technology because of a narrow and simplified gospel message. British sociologist Steve Bruce makes an insightful comparison between liberals and conservatives.

> Liberals . . . tend to see God's revelation as something which is always changing and which is best found in interaction, between people, and between people and their world. . . . Conservatives have an almost magical view of the ability of scripture to *act*, to work independent of the interest of the reader. . . . The

---

44. Schultze, *Televangelism and American Culture*, 54, 57.

45. Jacques Ellul offers a definition of "ideology": "The popularized sentimental degeneration of a political doctrine or worldview; it involves a mixture of passions and rather incoherent intellectual elements, always related to present realities." See Ellul, *Jesus and Marx*, 1.

46. Ellul, *Jesus and Marx*, 15.

47. Bruce, *PRAY TV*, 43–44, 46.

48. Bowler, *Preacher's Wife*, 2.

conservative preacher reduces everything to the need to preach the gospel and save souls.[49]

In global mission contexts, conservative theology has greater appeal for its offer of certainty. In reality, this results in a type of mechanical, reductionist conservative theology that is closer to Gnosticism than theism. It distorts reality into a two-dimensional, narcissistic battle between good and evil, Christendom and secularism, which is often proclaimed to be a "spiritual warfare." The perception of being isolated or persecuted by secularism further produces a confirmation bias when perceiving reality, pushing such a theology into further narrowness. Such movements seek to restore a past glory with today's saint-like leaders who claim to hold the Truth against a secularized, fallen world. As Eric Voegelin describes it, these repeated messages often serve to lead the audience into believing that the speaker must be someone who is upright and holy, and that only someone who is pure in heart can exhibit such a righteous anger at evil. Moreover, this charismatic leader promises a new vision that is especially desired in a corrupt world needing immediate renewal.[50]

Vision and Charisma

In early New England, church leaders adopted open-air evangelism as a strategy to counter existing ecclesiastical hierarchies. It gradually turned into a populist movement, where self-educated lay evangelists and theologians became very popular in America. Although few of them had received traditional theological training, these evangelists considered themselves the authority of religious truth. Swiss-American theologian Philip Schaff comments in the introduction of a book titled *Theology in America* that "every theological vagabond and peddler may drive here his bungling trade, without passport of license, and sell his false ware at pleasure."[51]

When it comes to evangelical entrepreneurship, many scholars refer to George Whitefield, colonial America's first celebrity, as one of the earliest pioneers.[52] With indefatigable zeal and pragmatism, Whitefield successfully appropriated commercial techniques and reshaped religious media

---

49. Bruce, *PRAY TV*, 46.
50. Voegelin, *New Science of Politics*, 135–36.
51. Cited in Holifield, *Theology in America*, 17.
52. Stevenson, *Sensational Devotion*, 163. Choi, *George Whitefield*.

into "products" that would appeal to the vast base of religious consumers in America. As historian Frank Lambert notes, "Whitefield's shipload of consumer merchandise symbolizes his immersion in a thoroughly commercialized society, one that provided him with the means of constructing a new religious discourse—modern revivalism."[53] His preaching style "borrowed from the theater techniques," and his use of print media "to generate buzz about forthcoming tours" proved to be effective.[54]

Among American evangelicals, the largely uncritical assessment of George Whitefield as "America's spiritual founding father" reveals the long-standing appeal of religious entrepreneurism.[55] Early evangelicals in America around Whitefield's time became archetypical pioneers for mass communication in the New World.[56] This "goal-oriented communications strategy" became the DNA of America's mediated evangelicalism. As Quentin Schultze analyzes,

> American media are distinctly evangelistic enterprises hoping to attract new "converts." The radio advertiser, broadcast producer, magazine editor, and newspaper reporter are contemporary evangelists. They are hoping to "win" people to their medium, to maximize ratings, to increase readership, to double market share, to champion social causes, to report evil, and the like. This kind of goal-oriented communications strategy, though now commercialized, grows out of a historic evangelical desire to conquer geographic space and win souls with the Christian gospel. Evangelicalism has always been organized around the goal to bring new converts into the fold and to expand its power and influence in the surrounding culture. Rhetorically speaking, the modern media are inheritors of the evangelical spirit so prominent in much of evangelicalism.[57]

There are some personality traits that are particular to religious entrepreneurs. Take America's successful televangelists in the late 1980s for example. They are known to be "pragmatic, self-made people who are admired for their savvy and determination."[58] Charismatic preachers are good at creating excitement and momentum. A contemporary example

53. Lambert, "'Peddler in Divinity.'"
54. Lee and Sinitiere, *Holy Mavericks*, 14–15.
55. Kidd, *George Whitefield*.
56. Schultze, "Introduction," 13.
57. Schultze, "Introduction," 13–14.
58. Schultze, *Televangelism and American Culture*, 11.

comes from Rick Warren, the founding pastor of Saddleback Community Church. In 2005, an article from the *New Yorker* describes how Warren "prophesied his way forward."

> Warren's publishers came to see him at Saddleback, and sat on the long leather couch in his office, and talked about their ideas for the book. "You guys don't understand," Warren told them. "This is a hundred-million-copy book." Warren remembers stunned silence: "Their jaws dropped." But now, nearly three years after its publication, "The Purpose-Driven Life" has sold twenty-three million copies. It is among the best-selling nonfiction hardcover books in American history. . . . Warren's own publisher didn't see it coming. Only Warren had faith. "The best of the evangelical tradition is that you don't plan your way forward—you prophesy your way forward," the theologian Leonard Sweet says.[59]

Nevertheless, the distinct traits of entrepreneurial zeal, pragmatism, and ambition of these religious entrepreneurs sow the seeds of both their success and later challenges. Canadian sociologist Lorne L. Dawson also points to the built-in instability of charismatic leadership. He describes such leaders as "romantic disrupters."

> A crucial feature of charismatic leadership is that it is non-institutional or even anti-institutional. . . . As Weber classically presented them, charismatic leaders are romantic disrupters who abrogate and transcend social conventions. They tend to break the existing patterns of authority or harness even older ones to new circumstances. . . . At the same time, they impose new demands for obedience and new standards of service and sacrifice, but they do so within an emotionally charged framework of relationships and activities. . . . Claims to charismatic authority by a leader and their followers can bring persecution from outside the group and lead to power struggles within the group, and both processes tend to aggravate the tyranny and instability further.[60]

Charismatic leadership may shape a church ministry in two opposite directions. Either they excel in authentically expressing the Christian faith and in caring for people in need, or they may devolve into "personality cults" that are "unfortunate perversions of the inherently human quest

---

59. Gladwell, "Cellular Church."
60. Dawson, *Comprehending Cults*, 154.

for authority."[61] As American historian John Wigger says, "[R]eligious groups have a way of elevating prophets beyond their abilities, a tendency made worse by our modern fascination with celebrity."[62] Many of these religious entrepreneurs believe and proclaim that they are serving God while unaware of mixed motives for realizing personal importance and organizational greatness. But more often, "as their organizations grow, they believe, so does their power to redeem the world."[63] For teams that lack integrity, this deep-seated spiritual pride plus their visible success for a time become a fatal deception for themselves and their supporters.

Here French social theorist Michel Foucault offers an insightful observation. When he examines the theme of governance in modern society, Foucault points out that the governing power among people by Christian leaders was arguably the source of modern social control techniques. He even terms it "pastoral technology." Throughout the Western world, the emergence of political rationality first came from the will to power of Christian clergy. It then was developed into the rationality of nation states, leading to the vicious norm of using power as a violence to dominate society.[64] Power is characterized by one's ability to control people's behavior. Christian clergy risk the abuse of power by making other people abdicate their wills and liberties. They often do so with eloquent persuasion and the help of religious technocrats.

The Rise of Evangelical Technocrats

For charismatic preachers to go from being locally respected personalities to national or international celebrities, they need a team of promoters. These are known as church growth consultants who actively identify strategic new techniques or markets for Christian expansion.[65] Just as a marketing team helps develop the products, a consultancy team often exists behind the scenes to help boost the popularity of a charismatic

---

61. Schultze, *Televangelism and American Culture*, 95.
62. Wigger, *PTL*, 337.
63. Wigger, *PTL*, 17.
64. Foucault, *Security, Territory, Population*, 135–216.
65. I use the term *church growth* in a general way. A specific use of the same term may refer to the Church Growth movement developed by missiologist Donald McGavran. My thanks to Michael Barbalas for pointing out this distinction.

preacher. These religious technocrats are the ones upon whom even celebrity pastors must depend.

Scholars of American evangelicalism have long pointed to the rise of the church consultant.[66] In helping a church to grow, consultants often promote pastors, books, films, and other goods beyond the church itself. *Church Executive* magazine in 2005 estimated there are a total of 5,000 church consultants in the United States.[67] These positions include titles such as director of missions and evangelism and director of church development. The phenomenon has also captured the attention of the *Washington Post*: "[C]ompanies in this field [consultancies] have been helping pastors incorporate multimedia technologies into Sunday services and use sophisticated marketing techniques to draw larger crowds."[68]

The rise of these religious technocrats fills in the void of late modernity, where impersonal systems permeate society and have replaced local knowledge and enduring ties of trust. As in other social domains, a technological bureaucracy has the opportunity to take central power. Furthermore,

> late modern society is complex and polycentric, with highly differentiated social spheres, domains or fields, each with its own characteristic and often mutually conflicting logics and characteristics. . . . [S]ociety is not subject to domination by one social domain and its power elite. . . . [They feature] the theme of individuals faced by impersonal systems.[69]

In a post-Christendom world, religious pluralism works for the advantage of these church growth consultants because wherever there is cultural unfamiliarity about Christianity, there is the potential market. Their job is to identify these markets that have not been saturated by the Christian message and "create new traditions" in these cultures. Here is a scholarly analysis by two sociologists:

> Recognizing that few people today identify strongly with any particular religious tradition, church consultants are creating new "traditions" out of the dust of suburban housing subdivisions and the savvy of market researchers. This is one of the reasons why the

---

66. Einstein, *Brands of Faith*, 60.
67. Quoted in Einstein, *Brands of Faith*, 60.
68. Cho, "Business of Filling Pews."
69. Riis and Woodhead, *Sociology of Religious Emotion*, 173–75.

fastest-growing local churches and television ministries are often independent of established denominations.[70]

These church growth consultants work closely with Christian preachers, translators, and technicians. Their ready-made programs and modules can be easily transmitted to another part of the world; they are then promoted vigorously and relentlessly. For example, American journalist and historian Molly Worthen describes how evangelical pollster George Barna popularized his seeker church methodology.

> He urged pastors to look to companies like Chrysler, which rebounded from the brink of bankruptcy by revamping its marketing strategy. Good business sense, Barna wrote, is biblical: "Jesus Christ was a communications specialist. . . . Notice the Lord's approach: He identified His target audience, determined their need, and delivered His message directly to them."[71]

Barna promotes a consumeristic model and argues that the Bible offers "almost no restrictions or structures and methods" for the church.[72] As evangelical theologian Michael Horton comments, "[N]ature abhors a vacuum and where Barna imagines that the Bible prescribes no particular structures or methods, the invisible hand of the market fills the void."[73] Infatuated with growth and size, church growth consultants treat larger organizations and wider influence as monuments to themselves. As Molly Worthen comments, "In the free market of American religion, where preachers survived by hawking their wares to the greatest number of people, head counts at the baptismal font—not the coherence of doctrine or the mastery of new knowledge—became the best of a church."[74]

American journalist and historian Frances Fitzgerald writes in *Cities on a Hill* that Americans have long followed a pattern of "starting over"—creating new religions, or perhaps better put, new versions of old religions. They made sure that religion in America reinvests itself in response to its social circumstances. This "quest culture" is a popular impulse that precedes the discovery of a new social trend. A social trend can refer to society's positive reactions to certain stimuli, whether it be a new type

---

70. Riis and Woodhead, *Sociology of Religious Emotion*, 14.
71. Worthen, *Apostles of Reason*, 156.
72. Barna, *Marketing the Church*, 37. Barna, *Revolution*, 175.
73. Horton, "Church after Evangelicalism."
74. Worthen, *Apostles of Reason*, 8.

of music, art, fashion, or religion. It is often created by a small group of people, but a larger part of society later follows. Mass media and communication have facilitated the creation of certain social trends. Today, many social trends are engineered by sophisticated marketing techniques. Christians are not unfamiliar with them.

In the evangelical world, public relations and media professionals are the trend-setters. The industry of Christian public relations is made up of true Christian capitalists. In 2006, the *New York Times* had an article on the life of Larry Ross, describing him as "arguably the top public relations man for Christian clients in America." He has served evangelical preachers and ministries that went down in American history.

> [Ross] sees himself as serving more than Rick Warren—or Billy Graham, or the men's ministry Promise Keepers, or films like "The Passion of Christ" (he has represented them all). The Kingdom of God itself is a client of sorts. Publicity, marketing and branding are his ministry. So the real question becomes, Why does God need someone to sell him? . . . Ross characterizes part of his job as finding the sweet spot where faith and the culture intersect, because religion on its own often isn't enough, as he sees it, to generate mainstream press.[75]

Religious technocrats in America like Ross unabashedly adopt such "generative" ethics. Contentment with obscurity and detachment from public glamor are simply not part of their moral vocabulary. With charismatic preachers asserting their manifest destiny, church growth consultants prepping the stage, and media relations identifying the new stars, a new evangelical movement is on the horizon. Their audacity to use all these "church growth" or "church planting" techniques and resources is founded on one deep-seated belief: Christianity needs to expand its influence in society, and God has prepared the opportunity structures. It is argued that there is nothing wrong with this kind of opportunism as long as it furthers God's kingdom on earth. As British scholar Pete Ward observes, "Church planting has become a way of growing the influence and market share of the congregation."[76] But the scandal of the evangelical mission is that in presenting a supposedly countercultural Christian gospel message, the proclaimers have created a counterfeit subculture that resembles secularism. The means (technique and entrepreneurialism) often subvert the end goal. Thus,

---

75. Saroyan, "Christianity, the Brand."
76. Ward, *Liquid Church*, 19.

Christian entrepreneurs began to produce a kind of limited mass culture, turning out sanitized copies of secular products, a season or two behind the times, like discount department store supplies shaping haute culture into American sizes. If secular business enterprises could market products promising self-improvement, how much better could Christian capitalists promote the religious equivalent. After all, as a number of Christian writers had claimed over the years, Jesus was the greatest salesman of them all.... In a sense, what these entrepreneurs were creating was not a counter-culture but a counterfeit culture.[77]

Personal charisma, novel techniques, and success-oriented pragmatism together make the launching pad of a religious brand. They do not automatically set the whole enterprise on an unfortunate trajectory. Other parameters might come into play and create a social psychology that leads to a predictable group behavior. Within a few chapters, we will see how behind the rise of each brand or movement is an evolving power structure that often leads to inevitable self-defeat.

77. Flake, *Redemptorama*, 22.

Chapter 3

Media and Reputational Capital

Then they said, "Come, let us build ourselves a city, . . . so that we may make a name for ourselves . . ." —Genesis 11:3–4

To Babel builders, the city-in-a-tower had great symbolic significance. Reaching to the heavens, it would make a name for them. They wanted to be known and remembered for generations to come. In the ancient world, one way to be remembered was to have children who carried on the family name. Or over time, certain people could gain fame by living an exemplary, moral, and wise life. Noah was an example of the latter. With only the word of mouth method of communication back then, concepts such as "popularity" most likely did not exist.

Name-making was also viewed as a kind of blessing from God. Shortly after the Babel narrative, God told Abram that God was going to "make a name" for him. This divine declaration was premised on a manifested humility and faith found in the chosen person. For the Babel-builders, behind the desire for name-making was insecurity; there was a fear of being scattered into obscurity. The pursuit of fame comes from that enduring existential restlessness of the human soul, the forever unsolvable anxiety about our own existence. Preoccupation with becoming famous might also be attributed to personal ambition, the search for meaning, self-worth, and even longing for immortality. Not only is fame a source of self-importance, but it is also perceived as protection from the existential predicament—the awareness of our own mortality. As American ethicist Stanley Hauerwas puts it, we need others to "acknowledge our existence."

> The problem at Babel is not human inventiveness; it is when our forebearers used their creative gifts to live as if they need not acknowledge that their existence depends on gifts. . . . It is not

technology that is the problem but the assumption that God's creatures can name themselves—insuring that all who come after will have to acknowledge their existence.[1]

Name-making can also be a defiance against death itself, for if this titanic project would prevail and last with their names on it, maybe the worth of these people would outlast death itself. Name-making may bring a sense of control and a force of domination. Babel serves as a medium to achieve this goal. The public fame of Babel leaders happened alongside group thinking. Brueggemann also reckons that the Babel project was achieving a "self-made unity" formed by a "fortress mentality." Instead of using the gift of common speech for authentic and unified worship, Babel-builders misused the power of human unity and cooperativeness for self-serving purposes. As commentator Bruce K. Waltke puts it, existential restlessness and an "appetite to possess" combine to produce such an act of defiance:

> On the one hand, people earnestly seek existential meaning and security in their collective unity. On the other hand, they have an insatiable appetite to consume what others possess. . . . The city reveals that the human spirit will not stop at anything short of usurping God's throne in heaven.[2]

Considering the above interpretations, Babel was a name-making media project through architectural signaling. Some scholars suggest its use of architecture as "a powerful media form"—its staggering height—was intended "to communicate humanity's impressive prowess and to signify its self-sufficiency."[3] In fact, the project was so impressive that even God recognized it in Genesis 11:6—"This is only the beginning of what they will do. And nothing that they propose to do now will be impossible for them." In the end, God also used "a media scourge," by imposing language barriers, to frustrate Babel.[4]

In today's world, leaders of Babel churches create a culture that lusts for fame. And fame delivers a kind of "reputational capital." Sociologists have long used terms such as social capital and cultural capital. The first refers to the value of social networks that bond similar people groups and

---

1. Hauerwas, *Christian Existence Today*, 48.
2. Waltke, *Genesis*, 182–83.
3. Byers, *TheoMedia*, 54.
4. Byers, *TheoMedia*, 54.

bridge diverse groups.⁵ The second denotes the value of cultural-symbolic assets of individuals (such as cultural habits, tastes, mannerisms, etc.) that promote upward social mobility.⁶ Along similar lines, the term *reputational capital* measures the value of intangible assets of individuals or enterprises granted by media publicity or marketing techniques. It also entails public trust. As scholars also point out, the higher the reputational capital, the less the costs of supervising.⁷ This high public trust then becomes a privilege that can be misused.

In the elevation of a narcissistic ethos embodied in fascination with fame and celebrity, we also observe superficial and transitory personal relations and the fear of mediocrity or obscurity. Religious entrepreneurs need constant stimulation—the next big project, another unparalleled media publicity—to boost their fame to the next level. They desire greatness and despise the mediocre.

The Industry of Evangelical Fame

Mass media form the rhetorical infrastructure of our public square in America today. We humans are like fish swimming in a mediated environment, which shapes our perception of reality. Mass media in their changing technological forms become extensions of ourselves. Not only are mass media ubiquitous, but they are highly commercialized. Communication is part of capitalism, which converts almost everything into commodities as media scholar Mara Einstein points out:

> Within this environment of being able to select your religion, or religions, combined with unfettered access to information, religion must present itself as a valuable commodity, an activity that is worthwhile in an era of overcrowded schedules. To do this, religion needs to be packaged and promoted. It needs to be new and relevant. It needs to break through the clutter, and for that to happen, it needs to establish a brand identity.⁸

Usually, a brand identity depends on the creation of celebrity personalities and stardom. To conservative evangelicals, "media are intended as a

5. See Coleman, *Foundations of Social Theory*; Fukuyama, *Trust*; Putnam, "Bowling Alone."
6. Bourdieu, "Forms of Capital"; DiMaggio, "Cultural Capital."
7. See Klewes and Wreschniok, *Reputational Capital*.
8. Einstein, *Brands of Faith*, 12.

conversion tool."[9] Here I summarize three major name-making media tactics by which evangelical brands achieve celebrity status. Since the third tactic builds on the previous ones, I will discuss it at greater length.

Appear on Major Media Platforms

The impulse of American evangelicalism for power shows in their rapacious use of the biggest "mics" in society: presidential politics, popular media channels, and social celebrities. Take televangelism in the 1980s, for instance. Televangelists such as Oral Roberts, Jim Bakker, and Jerry Falwell actively formed a coalition of electoral support for presidential elections.[10] As scholars point out, "[T]he recent swing toward political conservatism, escalation of the public debate about moral issues such as abortion and prayer in public schools, and the pervasiveness of television have created a favorable arena for these preachers to spread their influence and, for Pat Robertson, to run for the presidency."[11] By such engagement, televangelists have "acquired the notoriety normally reserved for movie stars."[12]

Other movements at many points in their life cycle have captured the attention of major media, such as the New York Times, Washington Post, Time magazine and the flagship evangelical magazine Christianity Today. These media outlets have also been in the industry of actively seeking new threads about emerging and newsworthy movements. So evangelical-media collusion takes place as a two-way attraction. One publicity piece begets the next big mic. For example, Colin Hansen, editor of Christianity Today, wrote a book in 2008 that gave the name to the emerging the Young, Restless, and Reformed movement. Afterwards, The Economist covered this trend in 2010, mentioning names of its leading figures such as John Piper and Mark Driscoll.[13] In 2014, an article on the New York Times again mentioned Mark Driscoll and John Piper, and added Timothy Keller, as leading figures of this "Calvinist revival."[14] Doug Wilson, a pastor from Idaho who had been a critic of mainstream evangelicalism, later through John Piper's endorsements in conferences, found his work gaining publicity in big media outlets such

9. Hendershot, *Shaking the World for Jesus*, 3.
10. Hadden, "Rise and Fall of American Televangelism."
11. Litman and Bain, "Viewership of Religious Television."
12. Litman and Bain, "Viewership of Religious Television."
13. "New Calvins."
14. Oppenheimer, "Evangelicals Find Themselves."

as *Christianity Today* and *Books & Culture*. These all helped raise Wilson's profile. Media publicity became an integral part of the ministries that gradually formed a subculture obsessed with "fame."

Join the Frenzy of Book Publishing

Publishing a book can get a preacher's name on the evangelical "Who's Who" list. As scholars observe, "Every few years, a book appears that becomes 'mandatory reading' within evangelical subculture. . . . [T]hese books create and are accompanied by a flash flood of marketing, videos, study guides, special editions, gift bindings, and seminars."[15] Examples include as the fictional *Left Behind* series (LaHaye and Jenkins, 1996), *The Prayer of Jabez* (Wilkinson, 1999), and *The Purpose Driven Life* (Warren, 2002). American scholar Daniel Vaca argues that "contemporary evangelicalism took shape and steadily expanded through commercial efforts to generate new media markets and build successful media corporations."[16] He also writes, "Through bookstores, supermarket checkout aisles, television talk shows, and more, a diverse spectrum of spiritual seekers have participated in the evangelical market."[17] Consequently, this evangelical consumerism has shaped a wide base of individuals who "rarely consume media produced outside of this world," which became a "separate and sanctified consumer space."[18]

If a certain book gets onto a best-selling list, it launches the author as a new star. Based on this fresh fame, a ministry gets its first boost of momentum. Celebrity pastors who gained fame through their books include megachurch preacher Rick Warren and YRR celebrity Mark Driscoll. Warren's *The Purpose Driven Life* and Driscoll's *Real Marriage* both made them *New York Times* bestselling authors. Joshua Harris, son of a couple who pioneered in the Christian homeschooling movement, gained quick fame by publishing *I Kissed Dating Goodbye* (1997), an iconic work of the purity culture among Christian millennials. The book was massively popular and sold over 1.2 million copies worldwide. Harris's subsequent books shared similar themes of what he called "humble orthodoxy." Later Harris founded the platform New Attitude Conference for Christian Singles. Reputation

15. Gallagher and Wood, "Godly Manhood Going Wild?"
16. Vaca, *Evangelicals Incorporated*, 3.
17. Vaca, *Evangelicals Incorporated*, 3–4.
18. Du Mez, *Jesus and John Wayne*, 8.

earned from these laid the foundation of these authors' later work as evangelical expansionists. Unfortunately, years later, the very books that made a name for Joshua Harris and Mark Driscoll brought about their downfalls, exposed by the same public media.

Launch Fame-Sharing Platforms

Some publicity-boosting platforms may also employ the terms "association," "alliance" or "coalition." Like popular concerts with multiple pop stars, these evangelical collectives favor a package-marketing strategy. Often a big-name celebrity pastor spearheads it, allowing his fame to cascade down to lesser-known preachers in the same bundle. As historian Kristin Du Mez writes,

> [C]onservative evangelical men knit together an expanding network of institutions, organizations, and alliances that amplified their voices and enhanced their power. Wilson invited Driscoll to speak at his church; Piper invited Wilson to address his pastors' conference; leaders shared stages, blurbed each other's books, spoke at each other's conferences, and endorsed each other as men of God with a heart for gospel teaching.[19]

In these and other forms of media exposure, evangelicals appeared to be unaware of how the means they used could compromise the integrity of their ministry. Their use of media had created a field of power, but their pursuit of that power was often cloaked by terms like "influence of the gospel" and "witness." As a result, to the American public, it became "increasingly difficult to distinguish margins from mainstream" and evangelicals who held competing theological understandings found themselves excluded.[20] It was through such deliberate media-marketing strategies that the field of American evangelicalism became a heightened sphere of conservative power.

On a larger scale, Americans in general are unreflective about the power of media in postmodern society. The approach is usually pragmatic and triumphalist. There is no adequate sociology of knowledge to guide their discernment. American journalist Tony Schwartz once gave an apt summary about the "side effects" of this unique sphere of human creation:

---

19. Du Mez, *Jesus and John Wayne*, 204.
20. Du Mez, *Jesus and John Wayne*, 204.

> The media are all-knowing. They supply a community of knowledge and feelings, and a common morality.... Media are both a door to the mind and a window to the world. They provide insight and "outsight"—the introduction to hitherto unperceived realities.... Godlike, the media can change the course of a war, bring down a president or a king, elevate the lowly and humiliate the proud, by directing the attention of millions on the same event and in the same manner.... The side effects of media . . . are often more powerful than the intended message . . . because the people who see and hear these messages do not see and hear them in the same context as the people who devised them.[21]

The pseudo environment created by media is more formative to most Americans than religion. As Pete Ward writes, "When we consume media, we consume people, and these people are celebrities, or rather they are transformed into celebrities as they participate in the process of production, representation and consumption."[22] It takes a counter-cultural alertness and deep reflection to see how we are easily consumed by media, instead of vice versa.

As previously stated, a populist following by the mass media also contributes to the rise of evangelical fame. Many churchgoers are zealous about attending large conferences with the latest famous speakers. Knowing who is who among the celebrity pastors creates a trendy topic of conversation. Along with one big name, there are a myriad of products for core fans to consume: books, podcasts, ministry websites, conferences, etc. Clubs of like-minded followers of a certain pastor begin to form, often via social media, creating a virtual community that likes to discuss the latest book or program of that particular star. Nationally and internationally, the church campuses of these celebrity pastors receive visitors who pay homage.

Populism runs deep in America, this land of new beginnings. According to American historian Nathan Hatch in his classic study of *The Democratization of American Christianity*, the genius of the American church has been its ability to integrate with the anti-elitist, anti-centralist appeal in popular culture. Evangelical Christians have always been searching for the next growth point, the next big stirring-up of the Spirit, and it is from watching populist trends with sizeable following that it achieves the goal. Scholars also point out that the democratic ideal and the upholding

---

21. Schwartz, *Media*, 4–6.
22. Ward, *Celebrity Worship*, 1.

of egalitarian principles may lead to a kind of artificial authority by way of popularization *per se*:

> Popularization created new social authority founded not merely on the charisma of the messenger or the authenticity of the message, but on the sheer distribution of the message to a lay audience. . . . Best-seller lists direct readers to presumably worthwhile books, while television ratings influence both network decisions about programming and viewer preferences. . . . Amid the great personal insecurity and social alienation in America's consumer culture, popularity enables individuals to identify symbols of authority and to participate in geographically widespread and culturally diverse social movements.[23]

Admittedly, not all famous preachers fall from fame to notoriety under the limelight. And pastors do need affirmation from their congregations. Some of them may have gained cumulative fame over a long period of time through tested character and performance in the public's eye. Many may not even favor program-centered ministry. A few may have even modeled quite non-controversial lives. But the creation of a vastly popular or influential public image by media coverage presents daunting risks for a church ministry to gravitate towards the direction of Babel. As Os Guinness puts it, "Size . . . is a critical factor in opening up a church to the temptations of modernity." The same can be said about American evangelicals' obsession with "Christian influence."[24]

Christian "Influence-ism"

Scholars have long pointed out that mass media in modern society creates a "pseudo-environment," an unreality that human beings insert between themselves and their external world.[25] Public fame of church leaders relies on these "mass-mediated representations of reality."[26] Contemporary mass media, especially Christian media outlets, are eager to dig out the latest "influential" leaders of the church. Sometimes, media publicity becomes a self-fulfilling prophecy because it actively helps create this kind of influence. Behind this alliance of personality and influence is the "close

23. Schultze, "Keeping the Faith."
24. Guinness, *Dining with the Devil*, 25.
25. Lippmann, *Public Opinion*, 10–11.
26. Schultze, *Christianity and the Mass Media*, 221, 293.

affinity between evangelical theology and American understandings of the missionary role of the mass media."[27] When media becomes part of everyday liturgy, it may powerfully change the Christian message. As Wade Clark Roof concludes:

> Television and film thus assume some of the functions traditionally assigned to religious myth and ritual. They are the cultural storytellers of modern society formulating narratives of good and evil, of hope and promise, at times reinforcing, at times redefining, the operative religious worlds in which people live. Visual media approach something of a Durkheimian community, creating "communities of interpretation" that shape and contest religious and ideological narratives.[28]

In a technologically controlled setting, mass-mediated Christian ministry risks impersonalism and false emotional attachment. Take televangelism, for example. As the author of *Spiritual Marketplace* explains, "Television adds seemingly real images to radio's intimate voices, providing an even more powerful means for establishing personality cults. . . . [I]t visually communicates one type of 'real' image better than all others: the human face."[29] This particular medium has the potential to create a "televisual intimacy." Children's television program producer Fred Rogers once also affirmed that television creates a connection that is "very, very personal."[30] Since Rogers was highly aware of his responsibility, he used this medium with considerable self-discipline.

Mass-mediated Christian ministry also risks misinforming the spectators and distorting their consciousness about the world around them. Because of the human cognitive tendency for reductionist simplicity, we as media consumers actually want to be informed of a second-hand reality, one that has been processed, manufactured, and packaged by journalists and experts. These are people who have what's called "public trust," a goal to which they aspire but are never able to entirely fulfill. Schultze puts it well:

> Propaganda is actually the result of mass society's insatiable but misguided quest for certainty, security, and power. People willingly seek simplistic slogans and join moralistic causes that embrace delusions and distortions of truth. . . . [E]ven religion becomes

27. Schultze, *Christianity and the Mass Media*, 48.
28. Roof, *Spiritual Marketplace*, 70–71.
29. Roof, *Spiritual Marketplace*, 76–79.
30. Quoted in Tuttle, *Exactly as You Are*, 41.

a victim of mass propaganda that feeds symbolically thirsty yet self-delusional audiences what they desire. . . . [M]uch of public life is now in the hands of priestly media professionals who naturally tend to their own interests and devise their own professional rhetoric as much as they serve the phantom public.[31]

Impersonalism creates moral hazards. Schultze emphasizes that because the public exists at a distance like a "phantom," media relations lack a crucial mechanism of accountability. Christian media sometimes make things worse because these are journalists who combine a missional fervor with an "informational fundamentalism," as some scholars point out.[32] They seem to wield the power of disseminating public information and act as priests and heralders of Christian mission and truth. Of course, these media want success stories, but once some movement gains attention, a symbiotic relationship begins between a movement and media. Christian media professionals may make up the third group of religious entrepreneurs ("trend-setters" in chapter 1) who practice the same utilitarian ethic. By their common efforts, evangelical Christianity is "obsessively preoccupied with [its] reputation, influence, success, rightness, progressiveness [or conservativeness], relevance, platform, affirmation, and power," as imprinted by its larger cultural climate.[33]

To be fair, mass media often played the role of the informed critic when it comes to corruption within churches in America and other parts of the world. But given the fact that religion reporters, whether Christian or non-Christian, are generally unfamiliar with the theological and power dynamics within churches, they often have trouble capturing the insiders' reality.

Celebrity Worship and Corporate Narcissism

The decline in religious institutions has left a vacuum that is filled by other social forces, such as contemporary media. This decline has not ushered in an expected secular age; "[i]nstead, celebrities were deified by fans whose religious impulses and hungers remain active in that cultural field that could bring out the best, or the worst, in them."[34] The emergence of celebrity figures

31. Schultze, *Christianity and the Mass Media*, 222.
32. Schultze, *Christianity and the Mass Media*, 295.
33. DeGroat, *When Narcissism Comes to Church*, 7.
34. Laderman, *Sacred Matters*, 64, 65.

has a religious or worship element to it. According to Quentin Schultz, "Americans like to turn ordinary people into heroes and celebrities. . . . No matter how critical the media are of some celebrities, the public thirst for them is unquenchable."[35] In contemporary American society, popularity or public fame is a form of "public praise."[36] It applies value or worth to someone's achievement in a certain social sphere. Peter Ward adds,

> Celebrity culture thrives on the fact that we take a view and we form a judgment. It wants us to take the moral high ground. From the *National Enquirer* and *Heat* magazine to the *New York Times* and the *Guardian* newspapers, the subplot of celebrity discourse is (im)morality. . . . Celebrities . . . function as symbols in the flow of communication.[37]

Fame brings reputational capital and power, and power has the tendency to corrupt. But how does it happen in everyday life? When does fame become a test of character? A concise answer is when fame makes us feel self-sufficient, entitled, and in control. Public fame is a test for the core of human ego. Unfortunately, narcissism is a genuine personality disorder that tends to plague many celebrity pastors today. Or one may also argue the other way around—narcissistic leaders often make great celebrity pastors. As Chuck DeGroat writes, "within churches a narcissist might even be described as charismatic, gifted, confident, smart, strategic, agile, and compelling."[38] Furthermore, he writes:

> Historically, Christendom's conflation of church and empire undermined the "kenotic configuration" of the church, replacing cruciform humility with hierarchy, patriarchy, and power. The grandiosity, entitlement, and absence of empathy characteristic of narcissistic personality disorder was translated into the profile of a good leader.[39]

Self-serving leaders and their budding ministries attract believers who revel in the former's false selves. On the internet, many victims of sexual abuses call their pastors and leaders "narcissists" with good reason. Increased self-consciousness can subsequently plunge almost anyone into

---

35. Schultze, *Televangelism and American Culture*, 33.
36. Schultze, *Christianity and the Mass Media*, 2.
37. Ward, *Gods Behaving Badly*, 23.
38. DeGroat, *When Narcissism Comes to Church*, 6.
39. DeGroat, *When Narcissism Comes to Church*, 21.

narcissistic self-obsession. Narcissistic traits of a leader show in an inflated sense of self-importance, a deep need for admiration and attention, and relatively low empathy for others. A narcissist may have great difficulty loving others before him or herself. Thus, psychoanalyst Sigmund Freud once said, "Whoever loves becomes humble. Those who love have ... pawned a part of their narcissism."[40]

Sometimes the active seeking of fame leads to self-destructive tendencies. Perhaps it is the reason some psychologists also call fame-making an act of "craze-making," hinting at its addictive quality. Many in the fame production industry reckon that fame is addictive. Here is a reflective statement from British producer Max Clifford:

> The sad part about [fame] is people that desperately need to become famous. It's like a drug . . . and there's so many people that come up and then they go, and when you meet them they are desperate, desperate for it. . . . They then become surrounded by people who live off them, pick off them[,] . . . who say what the person wants to hear all the time. They become wrapped up in fame and get a totally jaundiced picture of life and reality.[41]

The distortion of American evangelicalism by the consumerism of late-modernity is best manifested in the phenomenon of celebrity pastors who epitomize "the American preoccupation with stardom and celebrity status."[42] The term *celebrity pastor* is in itself a paradox. Narcissistic celebrity pastors are often motivated by a vision to change the world, but they cannot respectfully treat others as equals. They might appear caring and compassionate, but they use everything they can, including people, to implement the vision. They want united crowds to follow them, but they are also constantly alerted to who are with them versus who are against them. A narcissistic celebrity pastor, endowed with great spiritual gifts, homiletic eloquence, personable looks, and theological language, can become the most sophisticated manipulator. Such a person takes gifts of charisma for granted and becomes not merely self-sufficient, but rapacious for others' continued recognition of special status. While the term *cult of personality* is often used to describe the manufactured media image of political leaders, it has also been popularly applied to religious leaders who are celebrities

40. Freud, "On Narcissism."
41. Quoted from Griffiths, "Why We Seek." About the correlation between fame and addiction, see Rockwell and Giles, "Being a Celebrity."
42. Schultze, *Televangelism and American Culture*, 32.

in their own communities.[43] American historian Joel Carpenter sums it up as "the assimilative power of American popular culture."[44] American political scientist Corwin Smidt writes that "the old Protestant cultural emphasis on self-denial has weakened and an emphasis on self-fulfillment has become more prevalent."[45]

Another common characteristic of a narcissistic pastor is that absolutely nothing is his/her fault and he/she apologizes for nothing. The pastor takes a perpetual self-righteous stance, so he/she cannot be questioned. An article in *Relevant* magazine comments on the fall of grace of James McDonald, pastor of Harvest Bible Church, that being a celebrity pastor is about "branding":

> A celebrity pastor is a brand, and a brand doesn't take action against itself. That would be antithetical to its entire existence. Brands survive because they deflect damage, control the narrative, protect talent and promote new successes over recent failures. . . . Accountability is bad for brands. . . . The more people who affirm us, the more likely we are to believe them, and the more we believe them, the less likely we are to listen to other voices telling us less gratifying things. With this comes a dismissal of accountability—often in tiny increments—until you find yourself on a pedestal high above anyone who could give you an honest assessment of your life. It's a dark place for anyone to be. It's untenable for a pastor. It's ideal for a brand.[46]

According to Chuck DeGroat, "the missional fervor and rise in church planting . . . since the 1980s can be correlated with the growing prevalence of narcissism."[47] He further comments that nowhere is this dynamic more pronounced than among megachurch pastors. When a certain narcissistic personality in the leader combines with a Babel style of entrepreneurism, public fame becomes a spiritual temptation. To fulfill the demand of popularity and religious authority, celebrity pastors face the temptation to live a double life. There needs to be a gap between their public persona and their real personality. To a certain extent, this public persona needs to be

---

43. Schuurman, *Subversive Evangelical*, 195.
44. Carpenter, *Revise Us Again*, 240.
45. Smidt, *Pastors and Public Life*, 3.
46. Huckabee, "James MacDonald and the End."
47. DeGroat, *When Narcissism Comes to Church*, 8.

managed or "manufactured."⁴⁸ As Joel Carpenter points out, such "Dr. Jekyll and Mr. Hyde traits" are "very common among the most popular evangelical spokespersons of our day."⁴⁹

Evangelical consumerism creates a culture of narcissism rooted in the fear of failure in a post-Christendom world that marginalizes Christianity. Historically, the fear factor had been at the center of evangelical outlook about the world around them. As Kristin Du Mez puts it, "Generations of evangelicals learned to be afraid of communists, feminists, liberals, secular humanists, 'the homosexuals,' the UN, the government, Muslims, and immigrants."⁵⁰ This fear led to many evangelicals' decision to regain power and control in public life. With grandiosity and impression management at its center, Babel-type ministry risks fostering a collective narcissism. Narcissistic celebrity leaders and their followers form a strong codependent relationship, which is sometimes built upon an emotional system of rewards. Together they create a corporate narcissistic culture that boasts its orthodoxy or self-righteousness. Fame-obsessed, narcissistic pastors like to lead their churches down a fast-growth track. Therefore, size and public image reinforce each other to form an expansionist model. Often times, a coercive subculture has formed to manage the church's public image.

Impression Management

Socializing in a narcissistic subculture, church members are objects to be used for the selfish needs of the pastor. They are expected to fulfill duties, to invest time and money, not for their own spiritual nourishment, but to fulfill the ambition of the leader. Misuse of power in a spiritual context may lead to what is known as spiritual abuse.⁵¹ When events unfold that disturb a ministry's perceived "image, reputation, and legitimacy," an organization may be forced to manage its public image. In the case of well-known evangelical ministries, the stakes are high in terms of their own brand reputation. American evangelical scholar and advocate Wade Mullen offers a helpful analysis:

---

48. DeGroat, *When Narcissism Comes to Church*, 32.
49. Carpenter, "Contemporary Evangelicalism."
50. Du Mez, *Jesus and John Wayne*, 59.
51. Wehr, "Spiritual Abuse."

Evangelical organizations operating in a public light might find truth-telling or admission of fault to be fatal. This fear leads to a strong motivation to maintain a positive impression. Evangelical organizations might also argue that their use of organizational impression management tactics is motivated by a desire to protect the reputation of Jesus Christ. This mindset can add to the compulsion evangelical organizations feel to manage an impression.[52]

The term *impression management* was first coined by Canadian-American sociologist Erving Goffman, in his classic study *The Presentation of Self in Everyday Life* (1959). Goffman uses what is known as dramaliturgical analysis with the actor presenting a "front stage" image, which differs from the same person's "behind stage" version. Between the actor and the audience, there is a tacit agreement about what to expect and what to deliver. This motivates the actor to manage the public impression.

Impression management also takes place on an organizational level. It is intentionally designed to influence stakeholders' perception of the efficiency and legitimacy of the organization.[53] This becomes crucial to ministries that do not want to lose donors. Large donors, in particular, may become an important enabling group. According to an empirical study done by Wade Mullen, high-profile evangelical organizations (e.g., Bob Jones University, Sovereign Grace Ministries, and Mars Hill Church) might prioritize managing the image over "managing the problem" by way of media coverage and public statements.[54] During this process, Mullen observes, "the use of impression management strategies for the purpose of deception can cause an organization to become increasingly adept at using deceit, manipulation, and secrecy."[55] It reinforces a culture of tribal protectionism and cements a clan culture into the already malfunctioning system.

In sum, the entanglement of American evangelicals with media publicity tends to compromise the authenticity of their faith expressions. As communication scholars observe, evangelicals are very "predictable" when it comes to their responses to new media: "First, they praise the new opportunities to spread the gospel. They see God at work in emerging innovations. They rave positively about the evangelistic potential. They love

---

52. Mullen, *Impression Management Strategies*, 22.

53. Elsbach, "Managing Organizational Legitimacy"; Mohamed and Gardner, "Exploratory Study"; McDonnel and King, "Keeping Up Appearances."

54. Mullen, *Impression Management Strategies*, 22.

55. Mullen, *Impression Management Strategies*, 18.

to raise money to launch new media projects."[56] They also favor a business model by unabashedly using language commonly seen in the corporate world. For example, the founder of a megachurch is often called its "CEO." The global mission arm of a famous church describes its service as a "brand." When publishing a new book, a celebrity pastor announces the help of a public relations staff doing a "marketing blitz." Nevertheless, in an effort to expand influence and change the world through media techniques, evangelical leaders paradoxically enter into a process of alienation from true selfhood and the larger reality.

The step from evangelical entrepreneurs seeking fame to their congregations enjoying high publicity status in the media is crucial for generating the next "movement" that would attract more churches to join in or mimic their success. But step by step, architects of this tower of fame have almost invariably sown the seeds of their own defeat.

---

56. Schultz and Woods, *Understanding Evangelical Media*, 282.

Chapter 4

Engineering a Movement

> But the LORD came down to see the city and the tower the people were building. The LORD said, "If as one people speaking the same language they have begun to do this, then nothing they plan to do will be impossible for them." —Genesis 11:5

The artificial, celestial city of Babel, the step-like tower that manifested human creative prowess, was a visible success, at least for a time. Initially the Babel-builders seemed to have achieved their goal of keeping Babel as "the gate of God."[1] Even God acknowledged Babel's mighty potential. Leaders of the Babel-building endeavor evolved their strategies from technological innovation, rhetoric mobilization, and media projection to ushering in a movement of titanic scale.

When the word *movement* is used in common language, it usually refers to the threshold of a trend reaching a critical mass. For the past century, growth-minded Christian leaders favor the use of this word. To them, it implies visible signs of God's approval. It ranks them among generations of revivalists in history. Nevertheless, as Walter Brueggemann points out, the passage about Babel warns about our use of language.

> The (biblical) text encourages reflection upon language as a peculiarly important human activity. It raises important questions about how we speak and how we listen and answer. It asks about the quality of human communication and the function of language. The faithful community exists (among other things) to

---

1. Biblical scholars think that the name "Babel" comes from a Hebrew word that means "gate of God," and is similar to the word *balal*, which means "confusion." See Wiersbe, *Wiersbe's Expository Outlines*.

ENGINEERING A MOVEMENT

maintain a faithful universe of discourse against the languages around us which may coerce, deceive, manipulate, or mystify.[2]

In this chapter, I discuss in detail how the momentum of some evangelical movements was built. In doing so, I integrate themes from previous chapters into the analysis of each example. The fallout phase will be considered in chapter 5.

Power of the Evangelical Crowd

Leaders' use of "movement" language plays a significant role in shaping the social psychology of a group. In 1960, French scholar Gustave Le Bon's classic work *The Crowd* analyzed how a group of individuals may risk the morphing of their personal consciousness to a collective mind with "very clearly defined characteristics" that Le Bon refers to as "the law of the mental unity of crowds."[3] He further states that "in the collective mind the intellectual aptitudes of the individuals, and in consequence their individuality, are weakened" until "the heterogeneous is swamped by the homogeneous, and the unconscious qualities obtain the upper hand."[4] These social psychological processes take place in juries, electoral crowds, dictatorial regimes, and revolutionary groups as well as mass religious movements. As American social philosopher Eric Hoffer wrote, "all movements, however different in doctrine and aspiration, . . . they all appeal to the same types of mind."[5]

In America, although natural bonds of community have been dissolving with social apathy and atomization, purposefully designed campaigns can still draw a crowd.[6] It is even so in the evangelical world. Discontented with the declining power of Christianity in America, evangelical leaders and revivalists actively turn practical purposes into holy causes. Usually, with new techniques and an organizing medium, Christian conservatism and its orthodoxy can be repackaged into new products targeting different population groups such as seekers, families, young men, and even those who desire some theological intellectualism. Even in their active phases, these movements gradually shape their participants into collective thinking and

2. Brueggemann, *Genesis*, 103.
3. Le Bon, *Crowd*, 24.
4. Le Bon, *Crowd*, 29.
5. Hoffer, *True Believer*, xi.
6. See Putnam, *Bowling Alone*.

uniformity, instead of contemplation and reflection. It is no wonder that the evangelical mind suffers from an intellectual poverty in the midst of widespread enthusiasm or excitement, as Mark Noll famously indicates.[7]

Meanwhile, all mass movements follow a life cycle. After the active phase, no matter how long it preserves its initial creativity and enthusiasm, it often transitions into a phase of stagnation. The power of the crowd breeds its own dark side, manifested in blind faith, a stifling atmosphere, or signs of systemic corruption. The "creative destruction" impulse of entrepreneurism, according to Joseph Schumpeter, shows its craving to fill the void left by lost or deserted holy causes. Such a passionate activism is prone to recreate another new project, detouring deeper spiritual lessons of reflective contemplation. It is largely due to these cyclical features of the mass movement that there is often a rapid rise-to-fall trajectory.

Contemporary evangelicalism has seen many examples of artificial movements that follow a similar cycle. One after another, they emerged out of a response to a spiritual need in our times, such as the need for identity, community, and authority. Leaders utilized innovative techniques and made history-making proclamations. They catered to media-driven, starstruck crowds who craved and consumed everything their celebrity pastors produced—books, sermons, conferences, and coalitions. Media caught sight of them in a frenzy, initially elevating movement leaders to celebrity-status but eventually turning to expose the dark side behind the halo. Each movement had a rise-and-fall life cycle that left massive scandals that continued to tarnish the credibility of Christianity in the public square.

Televangelism: Fundraising Frenzy and Ministry Empires

In the 1970s, televangelism became a popular trend after television replaced radio as the primary home entertainment medium following deregulation in the media and broadcasting industry. From the beginning, televangelism depended on donations from its audience. New programs were designed to do fundraising among a large Christian population. Scholars observe that the programs were generally "fast-paced," "highly-entertaining," and full of "linguistic devices" and "persuasive speech."[8] Christian viewers were prone

---

7. Noll, *Scandal of the Evangelical Mind*, 3.
8. See Hadden and Shupe, *Televangelism*; Hadden and Swann, *Prime Time Preachers*.

to be misled by the many techniques used by televangelists to empty their pockets. A few examples follow:

> Super Savers used essentially six different fund-raising techniques. The first was selling sacred space: convincing viewers to buy a piece of the Rock of Ages. Generous donors could have their names inscribed on Oral Roberts's Tulsa prayer tower, on individually cushioned chairs in Robert Schuller's Crystal Cathedral, on chalets in Jim Bakker's Heritage U.S.A., or on "living memorial" bricks in Jerry Falwell's new Liberty Mountain prayer chapel. . . . The second tactic was selling prayer time, which could be almost as expensive as broadcast time. . . . Tactic number three was a more formalized version of the second. This was the join-the-club approach. . . . The virtue of belonging to these religious clubs—and indeed to video congregations—was that you never had to leave the sanctuary of your own home; you never had to shake hands with or smile at the undesirable and troublemakers who inevitably disturbed one's peace of mind at any religious gathering. . . . Joining a religious club also entitled one to become a souvenir collector. Accordingly, the fourth fund-raising strategy involved hawking holy molies.[9]

When the marketing ambition of many television preachers went out of control, these ministries created "more competition than the market could absorb."[10] Meanwhile, since their "insistence on linking highly particularistic political agendas with theological doctrine narrowed the base of potential support," the programs were bound to enter into financial disasters.[11]

Although one may attribute most televangelism scandals to a commercialized industry run by greed, there is more to it. Reflecting on the deeper causes behind financial malfeasance and fame-mongering, scholars point to the construction of unreality. They point to the "personal appeal" by television hosts as "the hard-sell strategy."[12] "Most shows fostered the illusion of intimacy, as the preacher zeroed in on that dear phantom lady with cataracts in Chattanooga, that hypothetical young girl in Akron who had been tempted by demons, drugs, and alcohol."[13] A 1986 study of linguistics also found that outreach by the medium of television has an inherent flaw when used as an evangelizing tool. One of the reasons is the fact that its

9. Flake, *Redemptorama*, 145–46.
10. Hadden, "Rise and Fall of American Televangelism."
11. Hadden, "Rise and Fall of American Televangelism."
12. Hadden, "Rise and Fall of American Televangelism."
13. Flake, *Redemptorama*, 145–46.

BABEL CHURCH

mere expansive reach was often conflated with the enactment or fulfillment of the Great Commission. Although televangelists tend to equate these two concepts with each other, they are two separate things.

> For televangelists the use of television is a matter of "fulfilling the great commission" of ensuring that every person on earth has the opportunity to hear the gospel. In keeping with their view of God as a very active participant in world events, television and other mass media are seen as God's provision of the means by which to carry out His will . . . Thus, one persuasive goal of televangelists is the proselytizing of their viewing audience, which they seek to extend throughout the world.[14]

These features of television as a medium, including emotional intimacy and the pseudo environment of global reach, have had cognitive consequences on the human consciousness. Viewers are more at risk of exploitation and manipulation when there is no accountability structure to check the power of televangelists.[15] The latter successfully created a sphere of power that bred abuse. Predictably, by the 1990s, scandals of celebrity figures such as Jim Bakker and Jimmy Swaggart brought disgrace to the whole industry of religious broadcasting after it bombarded the American audience with its version of the Christian message for decades.

Megachurches: Upgraded Sanctuary Experiences for Seekers

Megachurch leaders specialize in offering an upgraded sanctuary experience for seekers. This trend gained momentum in the 1990s. Later from 2000 to 2005, the number of megachurches in the US doubled, growing to 1,250.[16] At the same time average attendance at megachurches grew 57 percent, from 2,279 to 3,585.[17] Church growth consultant Peter Drucker is quoted as saying

---

14. Schmidt and Kess, *Television Advertising*, 35.

15. It is worth mentioning the Evangelical Council for Financial Accountability (ECFA) as an accountability structure. But given its voluntary membership, it remains a question whether ECFA has been effective in checking the trend of evangelical corruption. See Strickler, "Televangelists."

16. Megachurches also diversified into different types: program-based traditional mainline, charismatic and pastor-focused, and seeker-oriented ministries. But the characteristic elements in the use of techniques remain the same.

17. See Thumma et al., *Megachurches Today 2005*.

in the early 2000s that megachurches are "the most important social phenomenon in American society in the last 30 years."[18] These advocates for the megachurch movement offered a triumphalist description:

> America has seen an explosion in the number of megachurches over the past three decades. . . . The ministry activities and worship styles of the megachurches affect tens of thousands of smaller churches in the country and, thanks to the Internet, literally millions of pastors around the world. . . . Beyond the raw number and power of these churches, we believe that megachurches, their practices, and their leaders are the most influential contemporary dynamic in American religion. They have superseded formerly key influences such as denominations, seminaries, and religious presses and publishing.[19]

The success of megachurches can also be analyzed through their particular artistic genre. American theater arts scholar Jill Stevenson identifies it as "a unique, highly visible, and incredibly persuasive performative genre."[20] She terms its experiential strategies as an "evangelical dramaturgy," using a "synaesthetic space" to shape "the point of contact between worshipper and medium."[21] A physical, theatrical intimacy through artificially arranged space and events enriches or even replaces the individual's imagined intimacy with Jesus. A "devotional performance spectatorship" helps transcend the individual perspective into a "kingdom-size" view of other worshippers.[22] With these techniques, megachurches are bringing down heavenly worship scenes to earth; that is, "They sacralize consumerism through architecture, programming, and theology and effectively create an alternative Christian or church world in which participants live."[23]

Scholars compare these networks of megachurches as "specialized guilds" that provide specific and brand-named services.[24] Although many ministries set out with a nontraditional philosophy about institutionalized religion, they later "offer congregational leaders the kinds of resources

---

18. See Thumma and Travis, *Beyond Megachurch Myths*. About how Peter Drucker mentored young evangelical church leaders to apply marketing theories to church growth, see Nesch, *Church of Tares*.
19. Thumma and Travis, *Beyond Megachurch Myths*, 1–2.
20. Stevenson, *Sensational Devotion*, 162.
21. Stevenson, *Sensational Devotion*, 162, 166.
22. Stevenson, *Sensational Devotion*, 167.
23. Stevenson, *Sensational Devotion*, 167.
24. Stevenson, *Sensational Devotion*, 162.

traditional denominations offer."[25] For example, Bill Hybels's Willow Creek Association (WCA) attracted over 10,000 congregations from around the world to join it. This is roughly the size of the two largest Protestant denominations, making WCA a quasi-denomination. It functions in the mode of "influence" that is faster and broader, facilitated by new media technology. Accordingly, American sociologist Stephen Ellingson writes, this new brand of American Protestantism "wield[s] inordinate power."[26]

When explaining the trend, sociologists also point out that "It is likely not a coincidence that there has been a rise in charismatically led megachurches at the same time that there has been a surge in charismatic leadership in the business sector."[27] Os Guinness comments on megachurches' innovation as "using the insights and tools of the behavioral sciences to aid effective evangelism."[28] With typically charismatic celebrity pastors and a centralized leadership structure, megachurches are bound to create a "field" of power.[29] Evangelical scholars refer to megachurches as "total institutions" that " live in close proximity over a lengthy period and work together towards a single, shared, instrumental end."[30] The strength and danger lies in its "conflation of social spheres, with the collapse of these spatial, temporal and psychological arenas orchestrated and overseen via strictures of legitimized authority."[31] American evangelical author Andy Crouch describes this interpersonal dynamic:

> A friend was speaking with the pastor of a multi-thousand-member megachurch, one whose name is instantly recognizable in the world of evangelical Christianity. "How do you handle the power that comes with your role as a senior pastor?" my friend asked. "Oh, power is not a problem at our church," came the reply. "We are all servant leaders here." I believe it was a sincere answer—this leader's commitment to servant leadership is genuine. But I have been in rooms when he walked in and have felt the palpable change of atmosphere, as if someone had abruptly turned down

---

25. Ellingson, "Packaging Religious Experience."
26. Ellingson, "Packaging Religious Experience."
27. Corcoran and Wellman, "'People Forget He's Human.'"
28. Guinness, "Sounding Out the Idols."
29. See Bourdieu, *Distinction*.
30. Scott, "Revisiting the Total Institution"; Wade, "Seeker-friendly."
31. Wade, "Seeker-Friendly."

the thermostat and shut off the background music. He is indeed a servant leader, but he is also a person with power.[32]

Since around 2009, the media has begun to provide negative coverage of megachurches, including internal spiritual stagnation. The *New York Times* reported, "In 2007, leaders of Willow Creek sent shockwaves through the evangelical world when they announced the results of a study in which churchgoers reported feeling stagnant in their faith and frustrated with slick, program-driven pastors."[33] Though Willow Creek leadership performed a courageous move in publicly acknowledging its own weaknesses, the leadership emphasized that church members need to become "self-feeders" who rely less on the church.[34] In 2015, some scholars also questioned the claimed "newness" of megachurches: "by marketing themselves as a 'new social phenomenon,' megachurches received a great deal of media attention. . . . The media took the proclamations about the unprecedented nature of megachurches at face value . . . [due to] ignorance about religion on the part of the reporter."[35]

To this day, even after the many high-profile scandals, the megachurch trend has not entirely passed. Some have diversified and adapted into institutionalized models more like an ordinary local church. The media continue to describe them as "Christian behemoths" dotting the highways of American evangelicalism.[36] Compared to the transient fate of televangelism, which usually is a one-man show, megachurches have more ongoing appeal by diversifying programs and making "recreational Christian ministry . . . no longer isolated to camp meetings and city revivals . . . [but] part of the everyday life."[37]

Promise Keepers: Niche Marketing Masculinity

Promise Keepers' appraisal of institutionalized religion has been "less than sanguine, and its stance toward Christian churches seemingly more critical

---

32. Crouch, *Playing God*, 10.
33. Worthen, "Who Would Jesus Smack Down?"
34. Horton, "Church after Evangelicalism."
35. Eagle, "Historicizing the Megachurch."
36. Schuurman, *Subversive Evangelical*, 161.
37. Schuurman, *Subversive Evangelical*, 161.

than collaborative."³⁸ As scholars point out, by invoking rhetoric of evangelical masculinity, they advocate a "new form of power . . . [in] several interpersonal arenas."³⁹ Leaders of this movement "assume an entrepreneurial role in redefining masculinity."⁴⁰ "[They] attempt to adapt hegemonic masculinity to fit with demands for egalitarianism and male sensitivity within evangelical families, thus reinvesting modern masculinity with renewed vigor."⁴¹ Integrating authoritarian male leadership, militaristic language, and sometimes homophobic rhetoric, this movement attracted enough of a following to form a community of like-minded men who "inspire emotional outpourings and expressions of love between Christian men, encourage feminine surrender before God, and harbor a profound fear that men are weaklings and failures."⁴²

By 1997, the movement had expanded to eighteen cities. It had a rally at the National Mall in Washington, DC, attracting around one million men. That event earned the movement cover-page publicity in *Time* magazine, which named it as "one of the century's fastest-growing religious phenomena."⁴³ But a dubious line of comment also shows in small characters on the same cover page: "A new movement is filling stadiums with men asserting their manhood. This week they rally in Washington. Should they be cheered or feared?" Founder Bill McCartney declared after this phenomenal event that the organization would expand overseas, for he believed "God wants us to go global."⁴⁴

But as the movement gained momentum, more criticisms poured in. Many accused it of exclusionism, sectarianism, and ignorance of Christian doctrines. The organization also began to struggle financially. After Promise Keepers waived the registration fee for participants, only months after the culminating Washington march, this movement began to show signs of decline, mainly due to financial difficulties. Some critics say that despite this movement's narrow focus on conservative men and its strong activistic campaign feature, it became a transient thing. Since all movements have a life cycle, every emerging movement eventually loses much of its novelty.

 38. Bartkowski, *Promise Keepers*, 5.
 39. Donovan, "Political Consequences."
 40. Donovan, "Political Consequences."
 41. Donovan, "Political Consequences."
 42. Chapman, "Tender Warriors."
 43. "Promise Keepers."
 44. Abu-Nasr, "Promise Keepers."

Hoping for greater visibility, it came up with the idea of a millennial march with Promise Keepers men across the nation descending on capitol buildings in each of the fifty states at midnight on January 1, 2000. Leaders later cancelled the event and told men to remain home to face the threat of the Y2K bug. However, "Many wondered if the event had been cancelled primarily because it would have been an embarrassment, a testimony to the failing fortunes of PK."[45] Furthermore,

> PK lost much of its newsworthiness soon after laying off its staff and canceling its millennial march. In the blink of an eye, the high-profile media attention PK once enjoyed had evaporated. Gone was coverage of massive PK stadium conferences and the personal testimonials of lives changed that had graced the covers and feature stories of all the nation's top weekly news magazines. And front-page headlines captured so effectively by the group suddenly became a distant memory. Those left scratching their heads from diminished news coverage would see the writing on the wall with a quick glance at the numbers. . . . For their part, the Promise Keepers have not resigned themselves to being dismissed as yesterday's news. When questioned about their drastically diminished revenues and less impressive membership rolls, one PK spokesman glibly asserted that the group is merely letting "the soil rest" before reinitiating its harvest of men's souls.[46]

In 2001, the *New York Times* carried an article quoting sociologist James Mathisen, who had studied Promise Keepers for many years: "They grew so big so quickly, there was no way they were going to persist at that same rate. . . . In one way, they were victims of their own success." The same article refers to the organization's current theme as "Turning the Tide" and "extreme faith," referencing "a biblical verse about personal transformation" as well as "the popular culture's use of the word 'extreme,' as in extreme sports."[47] The impulse of speaking relevance to young men's familiar culture risked creating subversive narratives that challenge the uniqueness and authenticity of the Christian faith.

Promise Keepers has spawned countless authors who celebrate evangelical masculinity through their books. In 2001, for example, John Eldredge published the book *Wild at Heart*, which continues to celebrate the warrior-image of evangelical manhood. In recent years, evangelical rhetoric

---

45. Bartkowski, *Promise Keepers*, 3.
46. Bartkowski, *Promise Keepers*, 3–4.
47. Niebuhr, "Promise Keepers Still Draws Crowds."

endorsing ultra-masculine ideologies has revived, partly boosted by the resurgent conservatism in Republican politics. The ambition to revive PK to its old glory days has never died. Organizers now aim to relaunch its trademark stadium rally for men in the summer of 2020. They announced the plan to fill AT&T Stadium with 80,000-plus men for the two-day event. "The organization projects that up to 5 million more will participate via simulcast in as many as 30,000 locations worldwide."[48] As Promise Keepers Chairman Ken Harrison explained via a media outlet, "It really needed a new board and fusion of energy, a new vision. It has all these things now. Promise Keepers had to get back to the basics of what it was. . . . [W]e had to realize what is its brand and identity."[49]

Young, Restless, and Reformed: Refashioning Protestant Orthodoxy

The uniqueness of this fourth movement involves a reverse innovation by reintroducing Protestant orthodoxy to a younger generation. This does not make it less similar to other movements, especially when it comes to the use of media and publicity. In 2008, an editor at *Christianity Today*, Colin Hansen, wrote a book (*Young, Restless, Reformed: A Journalist's Journey with the New Calvinists*) that gave the name to this movement. In the book, Hansen also identifies the founding figures and central institutions where there has been "a significant Reformed uptick among students over the past 20 years."[50] But he also depicts the influence to be divisive: "Its exuberant young advocates reject generic evangelism and tout the benefits of in-depth biblical doctrine. They have once again brought the perennial debate about God's sovereignty and human's free will to the forefront."[51]

In 2009, this phenomenon caught the attention of *Time* magazine, which ranked the emerging New Calvinism comeback among young American evangelicals as one of the "Ten Ideas Changing the World Right Now."[52] During the next a year or two, media have repeatedly shone the limelight on this movement. The *New York Times* also published an article on one of the movement's stars Mark Driscoll, calling him "American

48. Tune, "Promise Keepers to Add Digital Reach."
49. Smith, "Promise Keepers to Relaunch."
50. Hansen, "Young, Restless, and Reformed."
51. Hansen, "Young, Restless, and Reformed."
52. Van Biema, "New Calvinism."

evangelicalism's bête noire," whose giftedness and success was shown in founding a neo-Calvinist megachurch. The fact that Driscoll was able to use the momentum of both the megachurch and YRR movement was a fascinating development.

> In little more than a decade, his ministry has grown from a living-room Bible study to a megachurch that draws about 7,600 visitors to seven campuses around Seattle each Sunday, and his books, blogs and podcasts have made him one of the most admired—and reviled—figures among evangelicals nationwide.... With his taste for vintage baseball caps and omnipresence on Facebook and iTunes, Driscoll, who is 38, is on the cutting edge of American pop culture. Yet his message seems radically unfashionable, even un-American: you are not captain of your soul or master of your fate but a depraved worm whose hard work and good deeds will get you nowhere, because God marked you for heaven or condemned you to hell before the beginning of time. Yet a significant number of young people in Seattle—and nationwide—say this is exactly what they want to hear.[53]

With YRR in the public eye, the movement and its stars have not been without critics. Historian Carl R. Trueman published an article identifying two pitfalls: "If leader-as-celebrity-and-oracular-source-of-all-knowledge is one potential problem in the YRR culture, then another concern is the apparent non-exportability of the models of church on offer."[54] He also worries that "a movement built on megachurches, megaconferences, and megaleaders" might do the church a "disservice" because "it creates the idea that church life is always going to be big, loud, and exhilarating and thus gives church members and ministerial candidates unrealistic expectations of the normal Christian life." As the *Christian Science Monitor* wrote in 2010, YRR challenged "the me-centered prosperity gospel of much of modern evangelicalism ... in an age of materialism and made-to-order religion, Calvinism's unmalleable doctrines and view of God as an all-powerful potentate who decides everything is winning over many Christians, especially the young."[55]

In 2010, the resurging wave of neo-Calvinism had attracted more followers from some large denominations, such as the Southern Baptist Convention (SBC). Even *The Economist* covered this trend: "Young Baptists

53. Worthen, "Who Would Jesus Smack Down?"
54. Trueman, "Nameless One."
55. Burek, "Christian Faith."

are flocking to conferences that feature Calvinist teachers such as John Piper of Bethlehem Baptist church in Minneapolis, or Mark Driscoll, a flamboyant, controversial pastor who leads Seattle's largest congregation, the non-denominational Mars Hill church."[56] Participants claim that they were "tired of a constant emphasis on numbers and church size." Now the new niche became "theological training and rigorous Bible study." The same article comments on the scale of the movement's popularity: "Some worried Baptist leaders claim that the neo-Calvinists are rewriting the history of the 165-year-old SBC.... The Baptists have missed out on other trends, such as the 1970s charismatic movement. They now have to decide whether neo-Calvinism is a movement they can safely ignore—or whether it may take over their church."

Since 2010, Presbyterian preacher Timothy Keller's Redeemer City to City ministry renewed the strength of the neo-Calvinist revival by spreading the "City Church" model globally. Keller spoke at the Lausanne Conference, and has since been disseminating a theory of the Gospel Ecosystem in the city, including prayer, evangelism, justice and mercy, faith and work and educational programs. This theory assumes that the gospel ecosystem, if built up, is in itself the remedy to the crisis of church growth.[57] By 2013, some media noticed signs of growth and division: "a growing number of 'new' Calvinists argue that, as part of God's blueprint for humankind, men and women have different roles in the family, church, and society."[58] It also mentions leading figures like John Piper and Mark Driscoll and how they have drawn criticism for interpretations on gender roles. In a few years, their promotion of complementarian roles for women in the church came to unfortunate fruition through the #MeToo aftermath in 2018.

In 2014, an article in the *New York Times* mentions Mark Driscoll, John Piper, and Tim Keller as leading figures of this "Calvinist revival."[59] It reports that "attendance at Calvin-influenced worship conferences and churches is up, particularly among worshipers in their 20s and 30s." This article pits this movement against earlier ones, such as the prosperity gospel and megachurches:

---

56. "New Calvins."

57. Keller, "Vision to Reach the City." See also Keller, "Introducing the New City Catechism."

58. Horton, "How Calvinism Is Dividing."

59. Oppenheimer, "Evangelicals Find Themselves."

That focus on sinfulness differs from a lot of popular evangelicalism in recent years. It runs contrary to the "prosperity gospel" preachers, who imply that faith can make one rich. . . . "What you'd be hearing in some megachurches is, 'God wants you to be a good parent, and here are seven ways God can help you to be a good parent,'" said Collin Hansen, the author of *Young, Restless, Reformed: A Journalist's Journey With the New Calvinists*. "Or, 'God wants you to have a good marriage, so here are three ways to do that.'" By contrast, Mr. Hansen said, those who attend Calvinist churches want the preacher to "tell them about Jesus."

Outspoken critics of the movement also spoke up through important media outlets. In 2014, as Carl R. Trueman pointed out in an article on *First Things*, "Calvinism . . . started to become a very marketable commodity and to attract big money."[60] Trueman describes this movement as "built on the power of a self-selected band of dynamic personalities, wonderful communicators, and talented preachers who have been marketed in a very attractive manner," and there can be a risk of no-accountability "where financial arrangements are opaque in the extreme, and when personalities start to supplant the message."[61] American evangelical scholar Roger E. Olson, author of *Against Calvinism*, also warns that many young preachers were zealous about stocking their church libraries with books by Calvinists like John Piper and Mark Driscoll. "They hold special classes on Calvinist topics, he said, and they staff the church with fellow Calvinists."[62] As scholars noted in 2018, pushback to the new Calvinists also came from inside the Reformed camp.

> A number of theologians have moved to defend more traditional articulations or orthodoxy, denying that the "new Calvinists" have the right to be identified as "Reformed." . . . Some of those reacting have gone further . . . to exclude from its ranks many of the most able and articulate defenders . . . , including John Piper, Mark Dever, and other members of such organizations as The Gospel Coalition.[63]

The fast rise to fame and controversy of the YRR movement finds best examples in two young celebrity pastors: Mark Driscoll and Joshua Harris.

60. Trueman, "Mark Driscoll's Problems."
61. Trueman, "Mark Driscoll's Problems."
62. Oppenheimer, "Evangelicals Find Themselves."
63. Caughey and Gribben, "History, Identity Politics."

At his most popular phase, Mark Driscoll, for example, was hailed by the media as one of the world's most downloaded and quoted pastors. *Preaching* magazine ranked him among "25 Most Influential Pastors of the Past 25 Years": "Reformed, emerging and controversial, Driscoll is a model for thousands of young pastors who read his books and listen faithfully to his podcast sermons."[64] Joshua Harris gained fame from his book *I Kissed Dating Goodbye* (1997), an iconic work of the purity culture among Christian millennials. Harris's subsequent books shared his passion for what he called "humble orthodoxy." Later Harris founded a platform New Attitude Conference for Christian singles. In 2004, he also became the pastor of Covenant Life Church under the Sovereign Grace Ministries (SGM), founded by a charismatic neo-Calvinist leader C.J. Mahaney. The scandalous fallout of Mark Driscoll and Joshua Harris will be a topic in chapter 5.

Dangers of Christian Social Engineering

Understood in its social and organizational context, American evangelicalism has been an ongoing movement in history. It has had moments of transformation, revival, institutional breakthroughs, and emerging communities. Momentum and fluidity coexisted to produce dynamic flows that sometimes seem noisy and contradictory. But evangelicals long to see the next new big thing, and this longing creates hopeful developments along with a risk for size-driven artificiality. Since the latter half of the twentieth century, church growth movements took different shapes, all showing certain enduring features, such as the publishing-conference-media approach. Korean-American missiologist Soong-Chan Rah terms it the "church-in-a-box" model.[65] At different points of time, emerging trends such as the televangelists, the megachurches and the more recent the neo-Calvinist movement (or YRR) became the sought-after models of "evangelical church success."[66]

To the Christian public, visible success seems to confirm divine approval, or at least laudable "influence." It then becomes infatuated with the illusion that someone has removed a certain marginality of Christianity in America. Many of these above-mentioned movements begin full of energy but then misplace their hope in techniques and communication

64. Duduit, "25 Most Influential Pastors."
65. Rah, *Next Evangelicalism*, 93.
66. Rah, *Next Evangelicalism*, 94.

technology, thinking the latter will be their servants. Unfortunately, instead, their enterprises become enmeshed in deep secularism and popular culture. Martin Marty foretold the pattern in the late 1970s: "Revivals usually breed reactions. Flows imply ebbs. The 'free ride' the culture has given all religion is not apt to last too long. The public finds many religious promises unfulfilled, and turns away."[67]

Another American scholar, Harvey Cox, also notes the love affair between conservative religion and media as the most significant trend in America.[68] Movements could not occur without media to popularize them. Acting in concert, movements and media have partnered throughout the "church growth" phases. As Os Guinness says, "Any movement that simultaneously hits *Time*, *Newsweek*, and *Christianity Today* and is viewed by so many Christian leaders as the best remedy for the church's ineffectiveness in the modern world deserves to be noticed, understood, and assessed."[69] Almost every movement went from being the media's new darling to a target of journalistic investigation. In each instance, divisions arose and interested persons fell into two camps: apologists or detractors. The end was great confusion to the detriment of the true mission of the church. Guinness also once commented that "many in the movement employ an uncritical understanding of modernity and its insights and tools."[70] He continues,

> through its uncritical use of the "new ground" of modernity, the church growth and megachurch movement has the potential to unleash a deadly form of idolatry and practical atheism in the churches. The result would be one more contemporary testament to the extraordinary power of religion that has no need for God.[71]

Polish thinker Zygmunt Bauman describes social life as embedded in the "fluidity of modernity," which is part of the trending pattern. Social realities "are now malleable to an extent unexperienced by, and unimaginable for, past generations; but like all fluids they do not keep their shape for long."[72] Modern society has witnessed "the creation of a kind of manipulability of

---

67. Marty, "Spiritual Revival."
68. Cox, *Religion in the Secular City*, 43–44.
69. Guinness, *Dining with the Devil*, 14.
70. Guinness, *Dining with the Devil*, 29.
71. Guinness, *Dining with the Devil*, 29.
72. Bauman, *Liquid Modernity*, 8.

the masses."[73] The habitual lack of reflection led to people's embrace of all things new and effective.

> [They] discovered that the key to spreading the Good News and increasing the size of their congregations was to blend the evangelistic and cultural mandates into the imperatives of Christian capitalism: find a need and fill it; find a hurt and heal it. Or as in Jerry Falwell's case, find a fear and sear it; find a hate and inflate it.[74]

On a much deeper spiritual level, the movements and fads exemplify traits of modern Gnosticism. Speaking of "Gnosticism," students of church history may recognize it as a theological problem in the early church. But according to German-American philosopher Eric Voegelin, Gnosticism remains at the core of the modernity crisis. He delineates six characteristics of the gnostic attitude that permeate many spiritual movements.

1. The gnostic person's dissatisfaction with the current situation.
2. The tendency in attributing problems to the world's poorly organized condition.
3. The belief that salvation from the evil of the world can be possible.
4. The belief in new order through a historical process.
5. The belief that human action can bring about salvational acts.
6. The construction of a formula for self and world salvation.

Based on the sixth criterion, elevating the technique (as a form of knowledge) to a salvific status is a central impulse of the gnostic. Founders of evangelical movements offer a certain formula for the church to revive itself as if it has control over knowledge about salvation.[75] It is also known as a "God in a box" approach, reducing salvation to a human technique. Pastoral charisma and spiritual authority, innovative techniques of marketing consultants, media's misused power in shaping people's consciousness, socially disconnected consumers with populist impulses—all these may combine to cause a "movement" to lapse into the perfect postmodern gnostic project.

---

73. Ellul, *Technological Society*, 370.
74. Flake, *Redemptorama*, 55.
75. See Voegelin, *Science, Politics and Gnosticism*.

Chapter 5

Scandalous Confusion

"Come, let us go down and confuse their language so they will not understand each other." So the LORD scattered them from there over all the earth, and they stopped building the city. That is why it was called Babel—because the LORD confused the language of the whole world. —Genesis 11:7-8

The Babel account has an antithetical parallel structure in the syntax of its original language. Everything that humankind proposed in the first half (Gen 11:3-4) was reversed and undone in the second (Gen 11:5-9). This chiasm places a divine act—"The LORD came down..." (Gen 11:5)—at the center of the Babel narrative (see page 76). It constitutes the turning point that moves the story from human actions to divine actions. Thus, we see the tower through God's perspective. As some commentators point out, "God's descent to earth to view the tower is no more proof of the author's primitive anthropomorphic view of God than is God's asking Adam and Eve where they were hiding in the garden an indication of his ignorance."[1] It is a moment of divine reckoning.

There is a recurring pattern in Genesis of a positive episode being succeeded by a negative fallout. For example, the creation of the earth, which was deemed very good by God (Gen 1-2), is followed by the fall and Cain's murderous act (Gen 3-4). The longevity of antediluvians (Gen 5) is followed by intermarriage of divine beings and the flood (Gen 6-8). The renewed covenant with Noah is followed by his drunkenness and the curse on Canaan (Gen 9). Here the gifting of common grace to tribes is

---

1. Wenham, *Genesis 1-15*, 239.

followed by the fallout of Babel. These all point to the poor stewardship of God's gifts by the human race.

A   "The whole earth had one language" (v.1)
B   "there" (v.2)
C   "each other" (v.3)
D   "Come let us make bricks" (v.3)
E   "let us build for ourselves" (v.4)
F   "a city and a tower" (v.5)
G   "The LORD came down . . ." (v.5)
F'   "the city and the tower"
E'   "which mankind had built"
D'   "come . . . let us mix up" (v.7)
C'   "each other's language"
B'   "from there" (v.8)
A'   "the language of the whole earth" (v.9)

The fallout of Babel presents acute ironies. What these builders deemed a solid and indestructible project was halted. God did descend to this artificial "gate of God," but with judgment, not blessing. What they prided themselves in became their downfall, and what they feared the most came upon them. They wanted great fame but reaped public notoriety. The narrative came to an ironic ending when God granted their wish for a reputation, but one hitherto known as "confused."

In a way consistent with the whole biblical narrative, what the Babel narrative intends to portray is hardly anything surprisingly new. As one commentator insightfully summarizes, "Genesis 11:1–9 . . . mirrors the attempt of humanity in the garden to achieve power independently of God. . . . [It] then has come full circle from 'Eden' to 'Babel,' both remembered for the expulsion of their residents."[2] The will for autonomy, which has always been at the center of rebellion, sets mankind on a self-defeating path. "Human cooperation, when it is fueled by autonomy and

---

2. Matthews, *Genesis*, 466.

directed toward self-interest, is shown by the story [of Babel] to be shallow, impotent hubris."[3]

From Movements to Scandals

The state of Babel's scandalous confusion in the public eye may resonate with today's American evangelicals as they watch high-profile leaders fall from their pedestals one after another. *Christian Post* summarizes this typical trajectory: "Often, the story goes like this: a 'celebrity pastor' with a wide sphere of influence falls prey to sin, leaving in his wake a trail of chaos and disillusionment."[4] This pattern also points to the uneasy relationship between American evangelicalism and mass media. Religious entrepreneurs need media and media is eager to document stories about celebrity personalities. This mutualism has created fame, erected new empires, attracted large audiences, and engineered movements. Chapter 3 examined the love side of this relationship. But as a Chinese idiom goes, "The same water that makes the boat float can also make it sink." The media are a double-edged sword. As Quentin Schultze points out, "Communication was both the cement that held the church together and the wrecking ball that smashed it to pieces."[5]

In the 1980s, two decades after American televangelists gained global fame, they were soon swamped in sexual and financial scandals.[6] The most notorious personalities that went down were Jim and Tammy Faye Bakker and Jimmy Swaggart. They left shadows on the powerhouse of televangelism. News about them appeared on major mass media such as the *New York Times*, *Time* magazine, *CNN*, the *Associated Press*, the *Washington Post*, and numerous radio and TV programs.[7] By now, public images of these celebrity pastors are marred with scandalous confusion.

Among the most influential mass-mediated evangelists since the age of television, Billy Graham was probably a rare one where no sexual scandals surfaced. Not only had Graham taken specific steps to curb against

3. Matthews, *Genesis*, 466.
4. Klett, "Leading Pastors Discuss."
5. Schultze, "Keeping the Faith."
6. See Wigger, *PTL*.
7. Schmidt, "For Jim and Tammy Bakker"; Ostling, "Jim Bakker's Crumbling World"; "Ex PTL Employee Testifies"; "Report: Former Co-Host Fletcher Says"; King, "Swaggart Says He Has Sinned"; Applebome, "Bakker Is Convicted."

temptations, he also helped found *Christianity Today*. He was active in the launching of ECFA, which specialized in accountability among churches. The one time Graham's image was tarnished happened when his taped conversation with Richard Nixon in 1972 disparaging Jews went public through the *Chicago Tribune* in 2002 and later *US News* after Graham died in 2018.[8] A fair criticism is that Billy Graham had promoted a masculine image and an affinity with political power that remolded American evangelicalism for decades to come.[9] Graham's help in winning evangelical support for Richard Nixon, and his later recanting of that position after the Watergate scandal, was probably the biggest public shame. Later what was left of Graham's legacy has been misused by his children for self-serving influence and embodies certain characteristics of Babel churches.[10]

When it comes to megachurch leaders, their public scandals show no patterns of concentrated eruptions because it usually takes up to one or two decades for them to rise to national fame. Notable leaders who stumbled publicly include Ted Haggard, Chuck Smith, James McDonald, and Bill Hybels. I hereby review each of these cases.

In 2006, Ted Haggard, founding pastor of New Life Church (since 1985), a megachurch with over 14,000 members in Colorado, made national headlines for his sex and drug scandals.[11] *The Guardian* describes Haggard as one who has gone on a "rollercoaster ride through evangelical power."[12] Previously, Haggard served as president of the National Association of Evangelicals. His quasi-denominational Association of Life-Giving Churches had over 300 congregations. After his fall from grace, Haggard moved on and started a new church.

In 2007, after decades of leading the Jesus movement,[13] Calvary Chapel, the founding congregation of a 1,300-church network across the nation, faced litigation and sexual scandals.[14] The litigation had to do with accusations against the leadership's financial mismanagement of hundreds of millions of dollars in ministry assets. As *Christianity Today* reported, "Chuck Smith, the founder of the movement, and his son are

---

8. Warren, "Nixon, Graham Anti-Semitism"; Warren, "Billy Graham's Troubling."
9. Du Mez, *Jesus and John Wayne*, 25–28, 33–35, 44–47.
10. Young, "How Franklin Graham Betrayed."
11. Serrano, "Evangelist"; Cooperman, "Minister Admits to Buying."
12. Harris, "Ted Haggard, Megachurch Founder Felled."
13. "New Rebel Cry."
14. Moll, "Unaccountable at Calvary Chapel."

battling in court with a former Calvary Chapel pastor for control of the Calvary Satellite Network's extremely valuable 400 radio stations."[15] A pastor describes the megachurch as "The *Titanic*" that has "hit the iceberg," but meanwhile "the music is still playing." Leading pastors revealed that Chuck Smith has been "dangerously lax in maintaining standards for sexual morality among leaders."

In 2013, the ministry of James McDonald, pastor of Harvest Bible Chapel (since 1988, SBC affiliation), with over 13,000 members, began to show signs of internal strife with members revealing "a culture of fear and intimidation."[16] Over time, many former Harvest members and staff have used media or blogs to detail McDonald's acts of bullying, sexual harassment, and misappropriation of church funds. Then in 2018, McDonald and Harvest Bible Chapel filed a libel lawsuit against two bloggers and a journalist. A year later, church members claimed that McDonald had wanted to hire a hitman.[17] After the scandals, Moody Publishers announced they would discontinue distributing McDonald's eighteen books.

Bill Hybels and Rick Warren are the two proto-creators of megachurches in America most often mentioned in the media. Of the two, Warren underwent comparatively minor controversies. For example, in 2006, the *Wall Street Journal* reported on how Warren's "purpose-driven movement" had created divisions among evangelicals. "Mr. Warren . . . has spawned an industry advising churches to become 'purpose-driven' . . . Anger over the adoption of Mr. Warren's methods has driven off older Christians from their longtime churches."[18]

Another controversy for Rick Warren was his 2009 "Letter to Uganda Pastors," that responded to an "Anti-Homosexuality Bill" by the Uganda parliament. He described the law as "unChristian" and called on Ugandan pastors to resist it. By then, Warren had become a global advocate in HIV/AIDS prevention, despite his conservative views on homosexuality. This cause may have motivated President Obama to invite Warren to offer a prayer at the presidential inauguration. In 2019, some media also broadcast news of Warren's hosting the authoritarian Rwandan president, which elicited public outcry from the evangelical community.[19]

15. Moll, "Day of Reckoning."
16. Devine, "Not Bluffing."
17. Blair, "Megachurch Founder James MacDonald."
18. Sataline, "Strategy for Church Growth Splits."
19. Do, "Rick Warren's Saddleback Church."

Peter J. Schuurman wrote in 2019 that experts on megachurch research agree that "5 percent of all current megachurch pastors will end their careers in some 'significant conflict,' including financial, sexual, or criminal scandal."[20] Though this statistic may seem comparable to other churches, businesses, or NGOs, Schuurman further estimates that "with 1,800 megachurches across North America . . . around ninety megachurch pastors' conflicts will most likely be covered in the media as their tenure ends." This means that the weight of each single pastor's disgrace will disproportionately affect the credibility of evangelical Christianity. The biggest fallout of the megachurch trend, of course, came during the #MeToo movement when Bill Hybels, founder of the Willow Creek Association and the Global Leadership Summit, faced allegations of sexual assaults that dated back to as early as the 1980s.[21]

With regard to the YRR movement, in just a decade or so, more than half of the earliest stars, including Mark Driscoll, C.J. Mahaney, and Joshua Harris, have heaped scandals upon themselves.[22] Because YRR relied on book publishing and forming alliances, the fallout shows a unique pattern linked to social networks. Not only did the star pastors fall from grace, but those who stepped up and vouched for the character of the accused celebrities also lost credibility.

Since 2014, Mark Driscoll had been facing complaints from church staff members due to his perceived abusive behavior.[23] Later it also turned out that Driscoll's *New York Times* best-seller *Real Marriage* had made it on the list because Mars Hill paid a consulting firm $210,000 to boost it there. *The Atlantic* commented, "Unlike the notorious televangelist scandals of the 1980s, however, there was no single disgrace or crime that brought Driscoll down. Instead, it was a series of accusations: of plagiarism, crudeness, a bullying management style, unseemly consolidation of power, and squishy book-promotion ethics, to name a few."[24] In 2014, *Forbes* magazine named Mars Hill "the Enron of American churches."[25] Timothy Keller still credited

---

20. Schuurman, *Subversive Evangelical*, 215.

21. Bailey, "In an Age of Trump"; Bailey, "Megachurch Pastor Bill Hybels"; Goodstein, "He's a Superstar Pastor"; Miller, "Misconduct Allegations."

22. Hafiz, "Protesters Call"; Shapiro, "Racketeering Suit Claims"; Dias, "Her Evangelical Megachurch"; Menzie, "CJ Mahaney Drops Out"; "Al Mohler Is Apologizing."

23. Welch, "Rise and Fall of Mars Hill."

24. Graham, "How a Megachurch Melts Down."

25. Asghar, "Mars Hill."

Driscoll with building up "the evangelical movement enormously," while admitting that "he has finally disillusioned quite a lot of people."[26]

Around the same time, the mishandling and cover-up of child sexual abuses in Covenant Life Church sucked both C.J. Mahaney and Joshua Harris into a gathering storm. At first, they gained the backing of many big names in the neo-Calvinist camp. But as the #MeToo movement prevailed over the next few years, their fame turned into notoriety. In the midst of the Sovereign Grace Ministries scandals, Harris first disavowed his views in the book *I Kissed Dating Goodbye* and discontinued its publication.[27] A year later, he made another announcement about divorcing his wife. As if these were not dramatic enough, a month later, Harris made a public announcement that he had deserted Christianity altogether.[28]

With the #MeToo movement, the interconnected networks of American evangelicalism suffered similar "corporate damage."[29] Exposure of sexual misconduct also shook the Southern Baptist Convention, but it brought about the greatest collective fallout of evangelical leaders. I will discuss this phase in greater detail.

Collective Fallout amidst #MeToo

In March of 2018, an article in the *Washington Post* stated, "Now some observers wonder whether evangelicals are experiencing a repeat of the scandals that led to the downfall of several well-known televangelists in the 1980s."[30] Scholars addressing the Evangelical Theological Society in 2018 also noted the unprecedented media storm revealing the hidden side of their faith community:

> Amidst the wake of the #MeToo Movement, the evangelical church was not able to vaccinate itself from the disease festering invisibly within its own body. . . . While thousands of individuals shared their stories of abuse at the hands of pastors and evangelical leaders, layers began to peel back, revealing pervasive patterns of denial, cover-up, and abuse of male power. Turbocharging the impact of the

26. Shellnutt and Lee, "Mark Driscoll Resigns."
27. Martin, "Former Evangelical Pastor Rethinks"; Klett, "Joshua Harris Says."
28. Parke, "Well-Known Christian Author"; Sherwood, "Author of Christian Relationship Guide."
29. Quackenbush, "Religious Community"; Griswold, "Silence Is Not Spiritual."
30. Bailey, "In an Age of Trump."

#MeToo movement on the evangelical church has been a series of investigative articles documenting abuse allegations against several prominent evangelical leaders in influential newspapers such as *The New York Times* and *The Washington Post*.[31]

Author and #MeToo advocate Mary DeMuth writes, "This is where we find ourselves today. Light is breaking through, but the darkness pushes back relentlessly."[32] Evangelicals never imagined themselves to be entangled with a sticky web of mass-mediated shame before. As author Andy Crouch writes about this stormy season for American evangelicals: "It was not a great week. In three separate cases in my immediate circles, a person with significant power at the top of an organization, each one a subject of flattering major media exposure during their career, was confronted with allegations of sexual misconduct and related misdeeds." He points out that "it is the system in which not just they, but we, are so deeply complicit."[33]

Crouch continues to describe the likely world inhabited by these sought-after celebrity pastors as one of public attention and private secrecy, distance, and unreality. The audiences of these church leaders have also been part of the fame-producing but reality-distorting system.

> It is the power of the one-shot (the face filling the frame), the close mic (the voice dropped to a lover's whisper), the memoir (the disclosures that had never been discussed with the author's pastor, parents, or sometimes even lover or spouse, before they were published), the tweet, the selfie, the insta[gram], the snap. All of it gives us the ability to seem to know someone—without in fact knowing much about them at all, since in the end we know only what they are, and the system of power that grow up around them, choose for us to know.[34]

Ironically, Crouch released a conscientious article through another fame-sharing media platform in the YRR movement, The Gospel Coalition, which soon faced its own controversies. The narrative of Babel shows us that sin can also cluster through a connectedness in fame-sharing, which acts as a buffer against accountability. Concentrated male power within this group was an equal predictor of its future trajectory. As Kristin Du Mez writes, "For all their emphasis on sin, New Calvinists seemed remarkably

31. Tracy and Maurer, "#MeToo and Evangelicalism."
32. DeMuth, *We Too*, 67.
33. Crouch, "It's Time to Reckon."
34. Crouch, "It's Time to Reckon."

unconcerned about the concentration of unchecked power in the hands of men."[35] The case of celebrity pastor C.J. Mahaney best illustrates this pattern.

As one of the most ingenious entrepreneurs in evangelical circles, Mahaney had successfully integrated the megachurch model with the YRR brand of orthodoxy. He later became the founder of Sovereign Grace Ministries, an association of eighty Reformed evangelical churches. In 2011, the *Christian Post* reported internal conflicts within Mahaney's church, with charges of pride and hypocrisy directed towards the leadership.[36] Then in 2012 a class action lawsuit was filed against Sovereign Grace Ministries, alleging Mahaney's cover-up of child sexual abuse. A year later, the lawsuit was dismissed. Since then, wide evangelical support for Mahaney through Together for the Gospel conference (also known as T4G) and pushback from the survivors network began a tug-of-war.[37] As one media outlet reported,

> [L]eading evangelicals are stepping up to defend Mahaney. "We have stood beside our friend, C. J. Mahaney, and we can speak to his personal integrity," wrote Al Mohler, president of The Southern Baptist Theological Seminary; Ligon Duncan, pastor of First Presbyterian Church of Jackson, Miss.; and Mark Denver, pastor of Capitol Hill Baptist Church in Washington, D.C. . . . But not everyone is rushing to Mahaney's defense. Boz Tchividjian, a law professor and executive director of Godly Response to Abuse in the Christian Environment (GRACE), which has investigated sex abuse allegations, found omissions in the pastors' statement. "Why no mention that CJ Mahaney was actually the Senior Pastor at one of these churches where all of this horrific abuse allegedly occurred AND that [he] discouraged these families from bringing this matter to the God ordained civil authorities?" . . . "This lawsuit is less about the abuse and more about an institution that took steps to protect itself and its reputation over the victimized souls (and bodies) of little ones," Boz Tchividjian wrote.[38]

So far, the story has not been picked up by major media. Only the *Christian Post* investigated and gave the victims' perspective.

> Pam Palmer, who attended Covenant Life Church for over 20 years, said that as a 2-year-old, her daughter was abused by a male

35. Du Mez, *Jesus and John Wayne*, 200.
36. Kwon, "C. J. Mahaney Takes Leave."
37. Bailey, "Evangelical Leaders Stand by Pastor"; Allen, "Abuse Survivors Want."
38. Bailey, "Evangelical Leaders Stand by Pastor."

teenager, and suggested that the church had its issues going to the authorities after hearing child abuse allegations. "One of the pastors told us, 'don't go to the police.' They had a lot to protect. They had money, power and prestige," she said, before ultimately going to authorities herself.[39]

The big names that appeared in support for Mahaney included three prominent Reformed evangelical authors, Justin Taylor, Kevin DeYoung and D. A. Carson, whose article on The Gospel Coalition blasted media portrayals of Mahaney as the "face" of the lawsuit against the Sovereign Grace network.

> Reports on the lawsuit from *Christianity Today* and *World* magazine (among others) explicitly and repeatedly drew attention to C. J., connecting the suit to recent changes within SGM. He has also been the object of libel and even a Javert-like obsession by some.... We are not ashamed to call C. J. a friend. Our relationship with C. J. is like that with any good friend—full of laughter and sober reflection, encouragement and mutual correction.... While the admission of friendship may render this entire statement tainted in the eyes of some, we hope most Christians will understand that while friends should never cover for each others' sins, neither do friends quickly accept the accusations of others when they run counter to everything they have come to see and know about their friend. We are grateful for C. J's friendship and his fruitful ministry of the gospel over many decades.[40]

This article also refers to the claims against SGM as a "conspiracy theory." Strangely enough, despite the affirmation of a strong friendship between C.J. Mahaney and TGC, only a year later, in 2014, the names of C.J. Mahaney and Joshua Harris disappeared from the website of TGC.[41] To people who questioned this change, The Gospel Coalition used a less congenial strategy—blocking questioners on the Twitter account of TGC. In 2016, American author Jonathan Merritt wrote in *Religion News*, describing TGC as "a towering, thundering goliath" that somehow felt insecure about criticisms.[42] "Its modus operandi combines harsh critiques of those outside it tribe with a bunker mentality that silences any who dare to question their thinking. While it presents itself as a resource for believers seeking

---

39. Lee, "Megachurch Pastor Confesses."

40. Carson et al., "Why We Have Been Silent."

41. Devine, "Mahaney, Harris Leave"; Weber, "C. J. Mahaney, Joshua Harris Resign"; Bailey, "Megachurch Pastors Leave."

42. Merritt, "Gospel Coalition."

to live their faith in a post-modern context, TGC is more like a case study in how not to engage culture."[43]

> TGC bloggers regularly express sharp disapproval of theologians, pastors, authors, and politicians using strong language. . . . Over the course of the past year or more, TGC has been on a social media blocking spree. Those who dare to criticize them are being shut down and shut out. . . . [R]ather than ward off internet trolls, TGC is simply silencing those who challenge them. The ministry has even taken punitive action against well-known Christian leaders. . . . You may not agree with popular blogger Rachel Held Evans, for example, but she is no troll. She's a *New York Times* bestselling author of numerous books and more than 100,000 people follow her on Twitter and Facebook. But Evans was blocked by TGC when she questioned a post on their site that used rather alarming language to discuss sexual intercourse. . . . TGC's blocking spree has swept in countless pastors, seminary professors, bloggers, and others.

In 2018, a reporter from the *Medium* continued to observe this blocking strategy. He compared TGC's scale of influence with its manifest gesture of arrogant intolerance in the public sphere.

> The sheer power and influence that The Gospel Coalition (TGC) holds is mind-boggling. . . . The TGC council boasts some of the most influential leaders in modern evangelicalism, including Al Mohler, Russell Moore, David Platt, and John Piper. We're not talking about small fish. We're talking about an organization with the financial means and influence to do whatever the hell it pleases. So, if you're Goliath, *why block the ant on Twitter?*[44]

The same article also explains the origin and growing influence of TGC: "The group is an online evangelical juggernaut that was co-founded by Timothy Keller, a popular New York City pastor, . . . TGC's online articles—which cover anything from Christian living to Bible and theology—generated 74.8 million page views in 2016."[45]

After this controversy about TGC faded, the SGM scandals continued through Joshua Harris, who was the young celebrity pastor of Covenant Life Church and mentee-successor of C.J. Mahaney. Harris was involved in

---

43. Merritt, "Gospel Coalition."
44. Sledge, "Together for the Go$pel."
45. Sledge, "Together for the Go$pel."

this controversy from the beginning. In one of his public statements, Harris expressed great sympathy towards victims by acknowledging that he had been sexually abused as a child. He said that some church members told him they planned to leave the church over the allegations. Urging them to stay, he said, "Please don't allow the circumstance to draw you away from faith in Jesus." Nobody would expect that in less than four years, Harris would be the one to step away from the faith.

In 2018, three years after he resigned from the megachurch founded by C.J. Mahaney, Harris made a documentary entitled "I Survived 'I Kissed Dating Goodbye,'" renouncing "the biggest accomplishment" of his life and announcing that its publication would cease.[46] *USA Today* had an interview with Harris that revealed how the change corresponds with his young and restless trajectory.

> I remember praying at the time: "God let me write a book that will change the world." I was young, zealous, certain, and restlessly ambitious. Youth, zeal, certainty and ambition—not unlike the ingredients of a Molotov cocktail which have a tendency to set the world on fire. And that's exactly what happened in my world of evangelical Christianity. My book went on to sell more than 1.2 million copies and be embraced by churches, families and thousands of single men and women. My ideas reshaped how many Christians practiced relationships and viewed sex. However, 20 years later, many of them look back with deep regret that they ever read it. . . . After listening to the stories and conducting a lengthy and sometimes painful process of re-evaluation, I reached the conclusion that the ideas in my book weren't just naïve, they often caused harm.[47]

A year later, Joshua Harris again became the focus of media by publicly announcing that he had split from his wife and faith.[48] *USA Today* quoted him as saying, "By all the measurements that I have for defining a Christian, I am not a Christian." He also apologized for remarks toward the LGBTQ community that contributed to "a culture of exclusion and bigotry." Historian Carl R. Trueman points out the only consistency of Harris's public image: media publicity.

---

46. Harris, "'I Kissed Dating Goodbye' Author."
47. Harris, "'I Kissed Dating Goodbye' Author."
48. Bote, "He Wrote the Christian Case."

While Harris seems to be making a clean break with his past, the style of his apostasy announcement is oddly consistent with the evangelical Christianity he used to represent. He revealed he was leaving the faith with a social media post, which included a mood photograph of himself contemplating a beautiful lake. . . . Life, it would seem, continues to be performance art.[49]

Trueman summarizes typical behaviors of YRR personalities: "savvy harnessing of fashionable idioms and marketing strategies, exceptionally clever use of social media, large and well-organized conferences, and professional-grade websites—all fronted by attractive personalities and brilliant communicators" despite "a fundamental lack of integrity." It is characterized by an act of "leveraging celebrity culture to do something for the gospel."[50]

Observers also need to consider a larger picture in which Harris's personal trajectory has been embedded: i.e., the ongoing Sovereign Grace Ministries sexual abuse scandal. In 2016, *Time* picked up where the SGM story was left and carried on the exposé.[51] But it was not until 2018, after Rachael Denhollander's advocacy against Larry Nassar won national attention, that this same woman used the media to expose the scandalous fallout of Sovereign Grace Ministries.

As *Christianity Today* reports, Denhollander "referred to the SGM saga as 'one of the worst, if not *the* worst, instances of evangelical cover-up of sexual abuse' and 'one of the most well-documented cases of institutional cover-up' . . ."[52] She spoke from her first-hand experience because the Denhollanders had been members of a church within Mahaney's network. The same article also revealed that "SGM evoked a religious freedom defense in 2013 when the confidentiality of its pastoral counseling was challenged." In her interview, Denhollander also offered a sobering observation of how pushback against #ChurchToo can be more intense than #MeToo.

> The ultimate reality that I live with is that if my abuser had been Nathaniel Morales instead of Larry Nassar, if my enabler had been [an SGM pastor] instead of [a Michigan State University gymnastics coach] Kathie Klages, if the organization I was speaking out against was Sovereign Grace under the leadership of [Mahaney] instead of MSU under the leadership of Lou Anna Simon, I would

---

49. Trueman, "Kissing Christianity Goodbye."
50. Trueman, "Kissing Christianity Goodbye."
51. Dias, "Inside the Investigation."
52. Shellnutt and Lee, "Sovereign Grace Disputes."

not only not have evangelical support, I would be actively vilified and lied about by every single evangelical leader out there. . . . I would not only not have their support, I would be massively shunned. That's the reality.[53]

Denhollander reaffirmed the same point to *Fox News*: "the way the evangelical church handles the issues of sexual assault and domestic violence is very much in opposition to Christ's teachings; it's an opposition to the Gospel."[54] She also lists examples of "institutional dynamics" whereby sexual predators have been enabled in various Christian systems. Fame is a factor leading to institutional protectionism. Or maybe institutional protectionism is another form of brand management because once a brand gains publicity, there will be a tendency to protect the brand. As Denhollander points out, "with evangelical churches . . . you have the reputation on the line and the perceived reputation of the gospel of Christ."[55]

The scandals and controversies following #ChurchToo in 2018 and 2019 did not just remove stars of American evangelicalism from their pedestals, but it also tarnished the credibility of many others who have busily formed alliances around these celebrity personalities. The media outlets that had anointed some of these celebrity figures now have turned around to pursue their stories of notoriety. To long-term observers of the evangelical drama, it can be a most disillusioning flurry.

Scattering: Gendered Speech through Media

Evangelicals are slow at discerning what the causes of #MeToo might be. According to a 2018 research project of twenty denominational-level church policies, 70 percent of the church guidelines describe sexual misconduct solely as an expression of sexuality, not as a misuse of power.[56] This explains why #ChurchToo soon developed into a heated debate over "complementarianism" versus "egalitarianism" on social media.

Historically, these two camps had a largely divided presence in fundamentalist versus mainline denominations. But in recent years, with the resurgence of Reformed theology, it has become a topic of heated debate within the Reformed evangelical circle. The former camp insists that

53. Shellnutt and Lee, "Sovereign Grace Disputes."
54. "Rachael Denhollander Discusses."
55. Lee, "My Larry Nassar Testimony."
56. Kleiven, "Sexual Misconduct."

according to God's order of creation, men and women play complementary roles in marriage and church life. So, women are not encouraged to exercise spiritual authority. For example, The Gospel Coalition has a confessional statement, claiming that "men and women are not simply interchangeable but rather they complement each other in mutually enriching ways."[57] The egalitarian camp, in contrast, consider the equal authority of both genders to have a biblical basis.

Since the 2010s, these became relevant issues for young converts to neo-Calvinist theology, a movement whose conservative appeal gravitated more towards complementarianism. Through their Twitter accounts, ministry websites, and public statements, a drama of theological debate unfolded in the public's eye. For example, the YRR movement leader and pastor John Piper attributes the egalitarian culture as one factor which caused Christians to forfeit "a great God-ordained restraint upon male vice and male power," promoting "complementarian" gender roles as the only biblical mode.[58]

It is important to first clarify these two concepts. "Egalitarianism" and "complementarianism" are two terms describing theological tendencies with regard to women's role in the church. The former affirms equality in authority and responsibilities between genders, while the latter considers men and women equal in personhood but with different and complementary roles in marriage, family life and religious leadership. In the 1980s, the Council on Biblical Manhood and Womanhood (CBMW), an association connected to the Southern Baptist Convention, was a main support base for complementarian theology. Wayne Grudem and John Piper are among the major theologian endorsers. Their co-edited book *Recovering Biblical Manhood and Womanhood* was listed by *Christianity Today* as "Book of the Year."[59] With support from conservatives within the Southern Baptist Convention, CBMW promoted patriarchal authority "as a nonnegotiable requirement of the orthodox Christian faith."[60]

Piper himself had been part of a controversial discussion in 2009 about whether women should submit to abuse. He encouraged women to "endure verbal abuse for a season" and "perhaps being smacked one night."[61] In 2018,

---

57. "Foundation Documents."
58. Piper, "Sexual-Abuse Allegations."
59. See Piper and Grudem, *Recovering Biblical Manhood*.
60. Du Mez, *Jesus and John Wayne*, 168.
61. Piper, "Does a Woman Submit to Abuse?"

while talking through a podcast for his Desiring God ministry, Piper blamed egalitarianism for leaving women vulnerable.[62]

Amidst the #MeToo social media warfare in 2019, fear of losing members to the egalitarian theological camp permeated the speech of conservative evangelicals who affirm complementarianism. The best illustration comes from the social media war surrounding the remarks of Beth Moore, a female evangelical leader from Southern Baptist background who in fact embraces complementary theology. It would be helpful to briefly explain the context.

Months after Moore tweeted reproachful messages in response to evangelical leaders' excuse of Trump's behavior towards women, Bill Hybels stepped down following accusations of sexual misconduct (October of 2018) and the Southern Baptist sexual abuse scandal broke out through the *Houston Chronicle* (February of 2019).[63] Then the news reported some problematic speech by Paige Patterson, head of a Southern Baptist seminary, which was ranked by media as "one of many that have rocked the evangelical church in the wake of #MeToo."[64] It was also during this same time that public statements by these accused abusers failed to satisfy the scrutinizing years of media. One article in *First Things* sarcastically points out Bill Hybels's unrepentant attitude.

> *Christianity Today* quotes words of vague assurance from the elders of Willow Creek Community Church, who promise to "walk alongside Bill in stewarding his season of reflection" and profess their commitment "to working together on appropriate next steps with him." I've never before heard the consequences of sexual misconduct charges described as a "season of reflection." This language downplays the accusations, as though pastoral abuse of women were just part of Hybels's spiritual journey. In his response, Hybels presents himself as a victim of circumstance. "I placed myself in situations that would have been far wiser to avoid," he said. "I was naïve about the dynamics those situations created. I'm sorry for the lack of wisdom on my part. I commit to never putting myself in similar situations again." He repents of being too generous, too liberal, too trusting of women in a working friendship. Given

---

62. Piper, "Sexual-Abuse Allegations."
63. Downen et al., "Abuse of Faith."
64. Burton, "Disgraced."

that at least seven women have come forward with complaints of misconduct, his self-evaluation needs to go deeper than logistics.[65]

This news wave emboldened Beth Moore, who was riding the #MeToo tide to become a voice for women in evangelical circles. She continued tweeting and castigating the evangelical movement, making manifest that her motivation for speaking up was the health of this community. As one article from the *Atlantic* comments, "Moore has not become a liberal, or even a feminist. She's trying to help protect the movement she has always loved but that hasn't always loved her back, at least, not in the fullness of who she is."[66] Readers need to be reminded that in June of 1998, responding to the growing crisis in the family, the Southern Baptist Convention in a national meeting of 8,500 delegates amended its essential statement of beliefs, the Baptist Faith and Message Statement, to include a declaration that a woman should "submit herself graciously" to her husband's leadership, and that a husband should "provide for, protect, and lead his family." This was only the second amendment to its Statement during its entire history, and its first-ever declaration dealing with a social issue.[67] This twenty-year span overlaps with *Houston Chronicle*'s report of systemic abuses that happened over the same period.

In 2019, at Southern Baptist Convention's *Caring Well* Conference, Beth Moore challenged the theological errors of the conservative camp: "Complementarian theology became such a high, core value that it inadvertently . . . became elevated above the safety and wellbeing of many women, so high a core value has it became, that in much of our [Southern Baptist] world, complementarian theology is now conflated with inerrancy."[68] Later in mid-October of 2019, Southern Baptist pastor John MacArthur publicly mocked Beth Moore at *Truth Matters* conference when questioned regarding his thoughts about her: "Go home." He followed up with another comment: "There is no case that can be made biblically for a woman preacher. Period. Paragraph. End of discussion."[69] This incurred days of heated warfare on social media. As the *Christian Post* reports:

---

65. Byrd, "#BillHybelsToo?"
66. Green, "Tiny Blond."
67. Quoted in Smith, *Christian America*, 160.
68. Briggs, "Beth Moore."
69. Smietana, "Accusing SBC."

[M]any took issue with the "mocking tone'" he adopted when communicating his perspective. . . . Moore received an outpouring of support from leaders in the evangelical Christian community. . . . Bestselling author Max Lucado said he was "grieved" over MacArthur's "derisive" comments, adding: "Are we, white, male, aged leaders of the church, listening? Are we heeding the message of our sisters in Christ?"[70]

American journalist and editor Katelyn Beaty wrote on *Religion and Politics*, pointing out the contrasting trajectories the evangelical culture expected of women and men leadership.

When MacArthur told Moore to "go home," he was not only going for cheap laughs. He was also implying that pious women will stay quietly behind closed doors, out of the affairs of church and public life. By contrast, male leaders embroiled in scandal easily reassume positions of spiritual authority. It's almost a cliché that a megachurch pastor who loses the pulpit over misconduct or toxic leadership will, in due time, set up a new church down the road. (Mark Driscoll, Tullian Tchvidjian, and Andy Savage are some recent examples.) Such is the durability of male Christian leadership.[71]

A critique by Kristin Du Mez more aptly sums up the pathological symptoms. These male leaders' complementarianism "was a vision that promised protection for women but left women without defense, one that worshipped power and turned a blind eye to justice, and one that transformed the Jesus of the Gospels into an image of their own making."[72]

With news headlines continuing to turn out stories about abusive pastors and ministries, conscientious leaders are grieving, lamenting and grappling for answers. Analysts point out common behavioral patterns of power-sharing, bullying, and manipulation. The public has seen time and again the ruthless silencing and shunning of #MeToo advocates and victims by pastoral figures whose job is supposed to be serving and protecting. Quite the contrary, these leaders have become so alienated from reality that they have lost something that is fundamental to humanity: empathy. Authentic voices often come from the margins of social media and spontaneously formed platforms. For example, a reflective blogger and clinical psychologist writes about why systemic abuse results from such alienation.

70. Klett, "John MacArthur Clarifies."
71. Beaty, "Behind the Rise."
72. Du Mez, *Jesus and John Wayne*, 294.

We talk about the abusers and harassers as people who hunger for power, or who are sexually addicted. But at the bottom of their actions is a deep and pervasive lack of empathy which sits at the core of every narcissist. These abusers have no feeling for the object of their abuse or harassment. They are entitled to sexual favors because they cannot put themselves in the shoes of those they abuse. The most fundamental aspects of human experience, those of empathy, sympathy, connection to others, is denied to them.[73]

Meanwhile, new books by #MeToo advocates are coming out with deeper analyses, warning the evangelical community of the danger when they do not hear the stories of victims. Survivor and advocate Mary DeMuth describes that this is why #MeToo or #ChurchToo has been "an unspoken and seldom articulated crisis."[74]

> [W]e have succeeded in wooing many through our front doors with relevant teaching; powerful, concert-like worship; and a myriad of family-friendly programs—with charismatic, celebrity pastors at the helm. Yet our painful, untold story is about the crowd of broken people flooding through our back doors, many of them women who have been victimized. . . . They are leaving because their brokenness is treated with contempt, inconvenience, or dismissal. . . . Leaders in the evangelical community have scoffed at survivors daring to tell their stories. They have minimized abuse, using rhetoric that morphs it from a criminal felony to a minor infraction—a sin issue to confront, not a crime to report. Some congregations have stood to applaud sexual predators. They have covered up abuse within their well-protected and powerful ranks and then embarked on shame campaigns against anyone who speaks out.[75]

Some #MeToo advocates celebrate the connectedness of mass media and social media that would help topple abusive ministry empires. But the futile irony is, they are also prone to forget the culpability of the mass media that pushed these abusive leaders to fame in the first place. It was American media that enabled or facilitated the deadly combination of fame, money and power in the first place. For example, according to the *Washington Times*, in the 1990s, Bill Hybels met with then-President Bill

---

73. Sinay-Mosias, "Narcissism and #MeToo."
74. DeMuth, *We Too*, 22–23.
75. DeMuth, *We Too*, 22–23.

Clinton on a monthly basis for over a year.[76] Ironically, both Bill Hybels and Bill Clinton later faced similar sexual scandals of preying on subordinates. The fact that Hybels's sexual abuse of women dates back to the 1980s shed light on how media has missed a dark side of Hybels's success story from the beginning. The reality of evangelical power abuse also seems harder to penetrate than White House politics.

---

76. "Clinton Sought Guidance."

Chapter 6

Global Epidemic

From there the LORD scattered them over the face of the whole earth. —Genesis 11:9

Insofar as missions rely on the wholesale faith in capitalist development, geographical imaginations that privilege the inherent virtues of the powerful—compassionate donors, heroic aid providers, devoted volunteers, and experienced teachers—they perpetuate the power-laden systems of inequality that necessitate, enable, and justify overseas missions, religious or humanitarian. —Ju Hui Judy Han

American theologian Stanley Hauerwas refers to the ensuing "Babel war" following God's linguistic confusion as the origin of tribalism. Having lost the common speech, Babel builders then "used their separateness as a club," and "the fear of the other became the overriding passion which motivated each group to force others into their story."[1] The tower of Babel was meant to be a cosmic center of religious worship with a global impact. But in the end, the impulse of missional expansion produced an epidemic of confusion on an even larger scale.

In history, missionary expansions from the Christian West to the Global South have always brought mixed blessings. Indeed, there has been genuine transformation of lives from darkness to light. But at the

1. Hauerwas, *Christian Existence Today*, 49.

same time, there have also been documentations of cultural superiority, ignorance or disruption of local power dynamics, and worse, perpetuation of abuses. The best example comes from the life of American missionary Katharine Bushnell.

Bushnell, an American medical missionary to China in the 1880s, never expected that her experience overseas would eventually subvert her long-held belief about the "advantages of Christianity."[2] While in Singapore and Hong Kong, Bushnell witnessed the appalling distortion of the missionary expansion project whereby indigenous women were mistreated "at the hands of Christian men." After an investigation, Bushnell concluded that the public prostitution system was entirely "the product of Western civilization," since such systemic abuse of women through institutions of public prostitution was "utterly unknown in China except in the treaty ports."[3] She attributed it to "the culpability of *Christian* men."[4] In her report written with another woman missionary Elizabeth Andrew, Bushnell pointed out that "it was the influence of Western Christian 'civilization' that exploited Chinese practices and fashioned the system of sexual slavery that had taken hold wherever the two cultures intermingled."[5] In today's globalized world, the experiences of Katharine Bushnelll are still very relevant.

"Good News" from America

As American political scientist Melani McAlister writes, "The history of American evangelicalism cannot be fully understood through a domestic lens."[6] She lists major forces in American evangelicalism shaping world evangelicals, including the US military's reach during and after the Cold War, American cultural-economic power, and the missionary enterprise.

> [M]any US Christians (and others) became acutely conscious of—and increasingly engaged with—the evangelical churches of the global South. And the members of those churches made their presence felt—attending conferences, publishing books, posting on Facebook, taking on denominational leadership roles, and

2. Du Mez, *New Gospel for Women*, 27.
3. Andrew and Bushnell, *Heathen Slaves*, quoted in Du Mez, *New Gospel for Women*, 79.
4. Du Mez, *New Gospel for Women*, 79.
5. Du Mez, *New Gospel for Women*, 83.
6. McAlister, *Kingdom of God*, 3.

sending missionaries to the rest of the world, including to the United States.[7]

For a very long time before the synchronization of world news by communication technology, Americans relied for information on missionaries, diplomats, and merchants. Prompted by the fundraising pressure, many missionaries who gained only superficial contact with local people groups and cultures tended to send back stereotypical and sometimes exaggerated reports. Sometimes as the only person out-posted by a missionary society to a foreign land, these letter-writers often lacked accountability for their communication.

In recent decades, when certain marketing teams of American evangelicals have gone to explore overseas market in less developed regions of the world where Christianity does not have a deeper imprint on popular understanding, they have relied on media communication to build up their "influence." But missionaries and Christian media continue to operate as intercultural interpreters with scant accountability structures built between two disconnected communities. Sometimes, particular pastors and their theologies were promoted because they were trendy or influential brands of Christianity in the West. This impersonal type of communication, without local knowledge of the pastors, exploits public trust from an indigenous population, fashions an artificial pastoral identity, and regenerates another movement abroad. Some of these imported celebrity pastors might have already been notorious in their local community due to previous fallout. As American columnist Walter Lippmann commented, individual Americans based their perceptions of other parts of the world, not on personal experience, but on the "pseudo-environment" created by mass media.[8] Back in America, these teams may churn out ministry reports with appealing but exaggerated content to get their American congregations to donate in support of global mission outreach.

Here is the key challenge: while globalization connects people groups and resources, it also detaches them from a local knowledge that is crucial to discern the missional integrity of a mission project. Not only are Babel church models exported as new brands of Christianity out of the more affluent part of the Western world (now North America), but celebrity preachers whose misconducts were exposed by America's free media might appear anew on an international stage with no dubious precedents known to the indigenous

7. McAlister, *Kingdom of God*, 6.
8. Lippmann, *Public Opinion*.

community. These "fallen" pastors can then get a new public image as an international evangelist. And with very rare exceptions, the media industry in other countries have little interest or capacity to expose the inconsistencies of these Western celebrity personas.

Take televangelism, for example. Scholars observed in 1991, "In Latin America, Jimmy Swaggart is far more popular than he is in North America. He is a virtual Protestant 'pope' who symbolizes to Protestants and Roman Catholics alike the rising power of evangelism in the region."[9] The problem is more sweeping than what concerns scholars—"people probably are converted more to American culture than to Christianity"— rather, a deceptive Babel church model has taken root in a foreign land. When Babel church models are transmitted from America to other parts of the world, a "globalization of false promises" takes place.[10] As British historian Brian Stanley writes in *The Global Diffusion of Evangelicalism*, "The battle for the integrity of the gospel in the opening years of the twenty-first century is being fought not primarily in the lecture rooms of North American seminaries but in the shanty towns, urban slums and villages of Africa, Asia and Latin America."[11]

Televangelism in Africa, India, and Latin America

In 2019, *Forbes* magazine ranked the Top Ten Richest Pastors in the World.[12] Every single one of them had a media arm. The surprising fact is that half of them minister outside of the US. Some African preachers' ability to obtain enormous wealth is a revealing fact given the income disparity between African countries and the United States.

---

9. Schultze, *Televangelism and American Culture*, 13.
10. Lule, *Globalization and Media*, 141.
11. Stanley, *Global Diffusion*, 247.
12. "Richest Pastors in the World." I thank Albert Stryhorst for this important content.

GLOBAL EPIDEMIC

Table 1. Forbes Ranking of Top Ten Richest Pastors in the World in 2019

Ranking	Name	Region	Net Worth	Ministry and Media
1	David Oyedepo	Africa	$150 million	Megachurch: Winners Chapel International, with 50,000 members in over 300 cities worldwide
				Media: author, publisher, owner of two universities
2	T. D. Jakes	US	$147 million	Megachurch: The Potters' House, with over 30,000 members
				Media: author, filmmaker, actor, singer, annual megafest
3	Chris Oyakhilome	Nigeria	$50 million	Televangelism: Healing School and Loveworld Books, with 40,000 members
				Media: TV stations, magazines
4	Joel Osteen	US	$40 million	Televangelism and megachurch: Lakewood Church
				Media: author (ten books on The *New York Times* Best Seller list), TV broadcasting
5	Enoch Adeboye	Nigeria	$39 million	Megachurch: Redeemed Christian Church of God, with over 18,000 branches in Nigeria
				Media: owner of a university
6	Creflo Dollar	US	$27 million	Megachurch: World Changers International, with 30,000 members
7	Kenneth Copeland	US	$25 million	Televangelism: Kenneth Copeland Ministries
				Media: author, TV

Ranking	Name	Region	Net Worth	Ministry and Media
8	Benny Hinn	US	$25 million	Prosperity gospel and crusade: Orlando Christian Center
				Media: author, crusades at large stadiums
9	T. B. Joshua	Nigeria	$15 million	Megachurch and televangelism: Synagogue Church of All Nations
				Media: owner of a TV network, largest social media following (3,500,000 fans on Facebook and 1,000,000 subscribers)
10	Joseph Prince	Singapore	$5 million	Megachurch and televangelism: New Creation Church
				Media: TV host, author

Another example is India. Historically, Christian mission in India has been influenced by the Syrian, Portuguese, and Jesuit traditions.[13] But in 2004, there was an unusual event wherein over four million people attended American televangelist Benny Hinn's "Festival of Blessings" Crusade in Mumbai. A year later, the same crusade attracted an audience of over five million people.[14] But Hinn soon found his luxurious living questioned by the media, and a state investigation followed.

> A new phenomenon is taking place in India today: televangelism. Propelled primarily by the global Charismatic movement, televangelism is shaping India's airwaves . . . As a result, some Indian churches have become replicas of success-driven, American, suburban, middle-class congregations in their organizational patterns: formulaic-worship styles and upbeat preaching based on the Charismatic ideals of health, prosperity and success.[15]

Media and culture researcher Jonathan D. James found that the church scene in India experienced a shift "with pastoral techniques resembling the

13. See Neill, *History of Christianity in India*.
14. James, *McDonaldisation*, xvii.
15. James, *McDonaldisation*, 1.

American model rather than the older models under colonization."[16] The sources of new influence seem to point to mass media, especially Christian television broadcasting. Scholars have also found that the growth of televangelism in Africa, South America, and Asia are in no small part due to the influences from America.[17]

The golden era of televangelism in Latin America happened in the 1990s after television sets became a popular commodity.[18] In July of 2011, Bishop Edir Macedo, one of Brazil's "most powerful televangelists" and "media mogul" as described by *The Guardian*, urged his followers to start a complete "media fast." Macedo has been leading one of the fastest growing and most controversial Pentecostal churches.

> Many suspect the move, however, is a tactic to divert followers' attention from bad press. . . . Macedo had called for "media fasts" twice past. On both occasions, the fasts coincided with negative stories about the Universal Church that were widely disseminated in the Brazilian media.[19]

The alliance between conservative evangelicalism, media consumerism, and electoral politics in South Africa, where around 80 percent of the nation professes Christianity, shares dynamics with those of the US. In 2010, the *Independent* reported on Rhema church, "South Africa's most influential church" with a 8,000-seat auditorium, led by Ray McCauley, who founded National Interfaith Leaders Council (NILC) to displace South Africa's Council of Churches.[20] The pastor proudly told the media that "the president comes to us to ask for advice; we are very influential and very active on social issues." The media also include outspoken voices who challenge the immorality of this church:

> The accumulating power of the evangelist has caused deep concern in South Africa's intellectual community. Jacques Rousseau, an academic at the University of Cape Town and the director of

---

16. James, *McDonaldisation*, xviii.

17. See Hadden, "Globalization of American Televangelism"; Maxwell, "Editorial"; Asamoah-Gyah, "Anointing through the Screen"; Gifford, *Ghana's New Christianity*; Lyon, *Jesus in Disneyland*; Smith and Campos, "Christianity and Television in Guatemala"; James and Shoesmith, *Hillsong, Benny Hinn*; Coleman, *Globalization of Charismatic Christianity*.

18. Garrard-Burnett et al., *Cambridge History of Religions*.

19. Phillips, "Brazilian Televangelist Tells Followers."

20. "Inside the Most Powerful Church."

the Free Society Institute, is among Mr. McCauley's more eloquent critics.... "We're living in a poor country and people are looking for a way out," says Rousseau. Rhema, he says, is exploiting them by selling an empty "rock and roll religion" with a US flavor that leaves no room for the "quiet voice of reason."[21]

A few of Rhema Church's publicists also hold government posts, and some had to resign over fraud allegations. The relationship between Pastor McCauley and President Jacob Zuma, who attends Rhema, also became controversial from time to time. The local press has dubbed Rhema the "Oscars church," alluding to the creation of celebrity stardom and their subsequent fallout. *The Independent* uses a tone of sarcasm to introduce their common notoriety:

> [According to] Mr. Zuma's biographer, the interest in evangelical Christianity is about political expedience, not faith.... Pastor and president have found common ground in the distance between their public statements on conservative morality and their rather messier private lives. Pastor Ray is on his second divorce, while Mr. Zuma is eyeing a sixth union. When the openly polygamous president was engulfed in a scandal over fathering children out of wedlock ... the NILC publicly forgave him.

For the above-mentioned reasons, although televangelism has largely squandered its popularity in America, it remains a trending ministry model in other parts of the world. The broadened use of the internet may have reshaped a hyper-competitive environment in America, but radio and television remain the major media infrastructure in many other countries.

Megachurches and Short-Term Missions in South Korea

The ties between American evangelicalism and South Korean Protestantism run deep. Korean scholar Ju Hui Judy Han finds that "the history of military and geopolitical alliance between South Korea and the US has had a profound effect on Korean evangelical Christianity, and that a sense of indebtedness to American generosity heavily influences the content and form of contemporary Korean missions."[22] Among many trends, megachurches are arguably the most visible developments in Korean public life. As media reports,

---

21. "Inside the Most Powerful Church."
22. Han, *Contemporary Korean/American*, 1.

The country is home to several of the world's biggest "megachurches," with hundreds of thousands of members, while conservative evangelical church groups boast millions of followers and enormous political lobbying power. Many star pastors build enormous personal fortunes and often pass control over their churches to their own children in a generational power transfer. But corruption or sex scandals involving evangelical leaders make frequent headlines, as do court battles over lucrative congregations.[23]

In 2015, the *Houston Chronicle* reported that megachurches, having been "largely a U.S. phenomenon," have started to spread around the world:

> An estimated 1,668 megachurches serve congregants in the United States, compared to 200 to 500 in the rest of the world. But many of those international churches see much larger congregation numbers than America's most popular megachurches. They mainly appear in Africa, Asia and South America. They thrive thanks to little competition from other churches . . . [24]

With a free religious market, democratic politics, and free media like the United States, South Korea, for example, saw an upsurge of megachurches since the 2000s. In South Korea, it often aligns well with a patriarchal, hierarchal leadership culture.

> In the design of the Korean mega-churches, it is stressed that the fundamental building block of the church should be a small, lay-led, home-based, homogeneous group. Organized along the lines of a corporation, firm or social category, members can progress through the subgroups of the church, and this represents a step in their social journey. . . . It remains to be seen whether the bureaucratic apparatus will stifle the life that it is supposed to assist and preserve.[25]

In South Korea, megachurch celebrity status is married to a patriarchal culture, creating a new symbol of corruption—hereditary succession of clergy power.[26] In October of 2017, Pastor Kim Sam-hwan, founder of one of South Korea's largest megachurches and self-portrayed "face of South Korean Protestantism," passed his pastoral position to his son. Korean media

---

23. "South Korea Church Scandals."
24. Levin, "Megachurches Spread."
25. Hong, "Encounter with Modernity."
26. Needless to say, hereditary succession also exists in America, but it is more common among para-church organizations. See Myong-sik, "Hereditary Succession."

reported that "the presbytery's vote to approve the plan flies in the face of a resolution banning hereditary succession practices adopted in 2013 by the general assembly of the Presbyterian Church of Korea (PCK)." It concludes this news with the comment that "the selfish secular reality of South Korean Protestantism is sad to witness."[27]

South Korea did have the media infrastructure to expose scandals from within its evangelical camp. In 2014, David Younggi Cho, founder of Yoido Full Gospel Church, was convicted of having embezzled $12 million in church funding.[28]

> Protestant megachurches, defined as those with at least 2,000 people in attendance every week, don't just operate all across the United States. This is a global phenomenon. Successful megachurches are operating in South America, Africa and Asia as well. And yet, no city has more of them than Seoul. The South Korean capital has 17 megachurches in all. Still, Protestant evangelical leaders in South Korea are facing a new challenge. Their public image has taken a hit in recent years due to a series of scandals, and the era of boundless growth for their congregations appears to have come to an end.[29]

Admittedly, the slowdown in church growth may be due to a variety of factors. The loss of integrity was one cause among many. There can be distortions other than size, control, and profits. As the largest mission-sending country in the world, South Korea has seen a development in its evangelical imagination known as reaching people in the "10/40 Window," a new strategy of "evangelism through mere presence" among "unreached people groups."[30] As a dissertation project shows, "the cartographic construction of the 10/40 Window and the unreached people groups produces the development of the Other, unreached by Christianity and global capitalism and underdeveloped, whose very existence legitimates the necessity and urgency of world evangelization."[31] No one expected that this world-making evangelical imagination would lead to a subsequent controversy that further tarnished the public image of Korean evangelicalism.

27. "Editorial: The Shameful Reality."
28. Bell, "Biggest Megachurch."
29. Bell, "Biggest Megachurch."
30. Han, *Contemporary Korean/American*, 123.
31. Han, *Contemporary Korean/American*, 126.

In 2007, news came that Korean missionaries were being held by the Taliban. The nine-day mission trip ended in a public ordeal with the release of all hostages except two, who were killed. The Korean hostage crisis brought lasting negative ramifications not only for the South Korean government to recalibrate its diplomatic relations, but all faith-based and non-government groups who had worked in Afghanistan for many years but had to evacuate. It infuriated many in the wider international relief and humanitarian community. Critics pointed out the missionaries' political naiveté and theologians described it as "the danger of the new popularity of short-term missions."[32] Popular criticism of this missionary project from Korean society caught Western media by surprise. *Time* magazine commented that the incident revealed "an unfortunate side to the evangelical movement in Korea" which is "increased competition."[33]

> Churches number in the tens of thousands here, and are competing so intensely for members that pastors feel pressured to engage in a kind of one-upmanship: sending congregants on as many overseas missions as possible. New markets and riskier missions tend to garner more publicity, which until now has translated into more kudos and ultimately more money for the pastor and the church.[34]

As Korean American evangelical author Soong-Chan Rah points out, "Korean churches were trying to outdo each other in radical, risky missionary efforts, in order to market their church more effectively."[35] The same consumeristic competition that contributed to Babel church projects in America is happening in South Korea. Rah laments "the propagation and the imbalanced cultural flow leading to a global church following dysfunctional patterns of the American church."

> [T]he seemingly unlimited capacity and potential of the Western church to propagate their ideas at a much faster rate, and the responsibility that comes with this level of power, needs to be examined. . . . The Western, white captivity of the church involves

---

32. See Robert, *Christian Mission*. Short-term mission by itself may not be the cause, for it can use a low profile and culturally sensitive approach.

33. Veale, "Korean Missionaries Under Fire." Also see "South Korean Hostage Apologizes."

34. Veale, "Korean Missionaries Under Fire."

35. Rah, *Next Evangelicalism*, 132–33.

the multiplication of Western models of ministry for export on a global scale. . . . [I]t has become a global phenomenon.³⁶

New ways of doing church are becoming popular in South Korea. One notable trend is "café church," seen by the *Atlantic* as "a counterpoint to the massive, hierarchical, institutionalized megachurches in a country where many are distrustful of major institutions, both religious and political."³⁷ The same article ends with an ironic twist by pointing out that some café churches in Seoul have been found to not report profits earned through their coffee shops. Even the grassroots movements that have sprung up to counter the "corruption plague" found in the Protestant establishment seem to be producing the same bad fruits.

Evangelical Masculinity in Asia

Scholars have studied how Western hegemonic masculinity is globally circulating, especially in regions where the forces of globalization have unsettled existing social structures.³⁸ Just as the increasingly unregulated power of transnational corporations places strategic leverage in the hands of particular groups of men, global mission may also have perpetuated the power of evangelical masculinity.³⁹ In Christian circles, men's movements emerged in regions other than North America. Take South Korea, for example. Since the 1997 Asian economic crisis, men lost jobs, leading to rising social problems such as divorce and domestic violence in homes where women focused on domestic work.⁴⁰ Both the South Korean government and churches launched campaigns and therapeutic movements to restore domestic harmony. One of the most well-known enterprise was the Father School movement founded by members of a megachurch in Seoul.⁴¹ Like the Promise Keepers in the US, Father School attempted to help men become emotionally and spiritually healthier fathers and husbands by aligning their masculine identity amid contemporary challenges. The *New York Times* likened it to a "12-step program," involving churches,

36. Rah, *Next Evangelicalism*, 132–33.
37. Strother, "Rise of Café Churches."
38. Kim and Pyke, "Taming Tiger Dads."
39. See Kimmel, *Misframing Men*.
40. Kwon and Roy, "Changing Social Expectations"; Oh, "16% of Korean Families"; Sung, "Familism in the IMF."
41. Laporte, "Korean Dads."

corporations, schools and other social institutions.[42] Scholars point out that "Father School draws extensively on the once popular U.S. evangelical Promise Keepers men's movement."[43] Additionally,

> Like Promise Keepers, Father School emerged around concern for a growing epidemic of "abusive, ineffective and absentee fathers . . . "with the goal of strengthening men's community roles through "healthy communication" and greater family engagement (Father School brochure 2010). . . . In a direct nod to Promise Keepers, Father School requires participants to wear the same style of blue-and-white striped "referee" uniforms worn by Promise Keepers members.

But unlike the Promise Keepers, Father School also developed its non-religious and inclusive programs to accommodate non-Christian and multicultural families.[44] The movement also developed its own unique techniques of community building, such as hugging rituals and the writing of "confessional" letters to family members. Despite its wide influence, critics point out that since Father School draws on images of Euro-American men, they tended to suggest "a distinctly American form of hegemonic masculinity."[45]

> [T]he rhetoric of Father School leaders and documents indicates the reproduction of "Orientalist" views promulgated in the United States. Specially, Asian cultures are cast as backward, gender traditional, and slow to change and Asian parents as authoritarian, emotionally distant "Tiger" moms and dads . . . Father School glorifies Euro-American masculinity as a superior example to emulate. . . . [Its] teachings thus provide evidence of the emerging dominance of the hegemonic masculinity associated with Western society.

Father School leaders have used videos of the Promise Keepers gathering where men were shown hugging, confessing, and holding hands in prayer. As researchers who did participant observation studies noticed, Father School leaders never inform participants that the Promise Keepers enterprise rapidly declined within a few years of its initiation. Only a few participants who had lived in the United States voiced the strongest critique of promoting such white American masculinity. Korean scholar Nami Kum

42. Chung, "I Learned That the Happiness"; Park, "Multicultural Father School."
43. Kim and Pyke, "Taming Tiger Dads."
44. Lee and Kang, "Development of Father School."
45. Connell, "Change among the Gatekeepers."

also pointed out that, although Father School sought to promote a cultural shift "from the authoritarian patriarch to the 'benevolent' patriarch of the family," no qualitative changes were made in gender roles.[46] "By reconfiguring patriarchy as a benevolent system, Father School further strengthens patriarchy instead of destabilizing it."[47] The movement's inability to address larger institutional structures in society that shape Korean families proves to be a contradiction in both rhetoric and practice.

Christian ministry that promotes evangelical masculinity has also appealed to the Chinese church. For example, in 2018, *Overseas Campus*, a Chinese-language Christian magazine that enjoys the largest circulation in Chinese-speaking communities covered the Promise Keepers movement.[48] It applauds PK events in Detroit and Los Angeles, ending the commendation with a call for repentance for secular America. Other Chinese-language media such as *Good TV News*, *Christian Times*, and *Christian Weekly* also reported this "renewed men's movement."

Other brands of American evangelicalism promoting masculinity and domination of females have also appealed to the Chinese Christian community. By publishing books in translation, some even expanded to mainland China, now one of the world's biggest religious markets. In 2011, *Created to Be His Helpmeet* by Debi Pearl was published and became popular among urban Christians. Many pastors recommended it to their church members. Book clubs formed to discuss it. Its fundamentalist theology latches onto the overarching tone of submission in Chinese culture. It was not until a few years later that many readers began to post challenging comments on book review websites with regard to the book's theology. Very few of them were aware that by 2011, the ministry of Debi Pearl had been questioned by Western media such as the *New York Times* and *Christianity Today*, initially on the grounds of child abuse.

By 2011, according to the *New York Times*, Michael and Debi Pearl's self-published book *To Train Up A Child* sold more than 670,000 copies in America.[49] It includes instructions on how to physically punish children's misbehavior. The Pearls's No Greater Joy Ministries website says that "Proper application of the rod is indispensable to communicating the divine principle of retributive justice," and that people who avoid using the rod might be

46. Kum, *Gendered Politics*, xiii.
47. Kum, *Gendered Politics*, xiii.
48. Yue, "Only for Men."
49. Eckholm, "Preaching Virtue of Spanking."

"emotional coward[s]."[50] Medical experts told the *New York Times* that they are concerned about how the Pearl methods promote child abuse. Media associate these teachings with three incidents of child deaths in homeschooling families. "All the parents cited as influence the teachings of No Greater Joy Ministries," reports *Christianity Today*.[51] In response, Michael Pearl told the *National Post* that "[media] have created a profile of abuse and they are searching for someone to fill their preconceived image."[52] Critics also think that Debi Pearl's book *Created to Be His Helpmeet* continues her endorsement of domestic abuse. Evangelical author Rachel Held Evans sounded the alarm, writing, "This is not simply a matter of different parenting methods or relationship styles; it is a matter of abuse."[53]

In 2014, when Bill Gothard, founder of the Institute in Basic Life Principles, was confronted by allegations of sexual harassment and molestation and stepped down from leadership,[54] victims posted on Facebook, saying, "I just rejoiced to see that huge ministry fall and I helped." In response to this controversy, Debi Pearl rose to Gothard's defense. She blogged on the No Greater Joy website, "This attack was not initiated to right an ongoing wrong or to establish justice and purity; the critics have unwittingly joined the last-days, Satanic attack on God's people to denigrate the very name of Christ."[55]

Young, Restless, and Reformed in China

When it comes to Christian mission in China, Western media have been interested in covering a growing Christian population under an atheistic communist regime. Some scholars in the field of Chinese Christianity also exploit the opportunity by resorting to a doubling up of the revival and persecution narratives. The media's tendency to grant moral legitimacy to any individuals or institutions that resist the communist regime has created a confirmation bias—these communist resisters can only be praised publicly for their activism but not held accountable for their own abuse of power.

50. Quoted in Hayes, "Is Conservative Christian Group."
51. Strong, "When Child Discipline Becomes Abuse."
52. Bosesveld, "Q&A with Michael Pearl."
53. Evans, "Abusive Teachings."
54. Knowles, "Leader of Oak Brook."
55. Pearl, "Debi Pearl Weighs In."

The YRR movement had officially come to mainland China through the translated works by John Piper, D. A. Carson, and Timothy Keller. Public records show that one of these high-profile churches, Early Rain Reformed Presbyterian Church (Chengdu since 2008), had been included in Timothy Keller's City to City training since 2010.[56] This church then became another branch of Keller's ministry network in mainland China through a mission organization connected with the Presbyterian Church of America.[57] Since 2016, Christian media and scholarship have noticed the emergence of "high-profile urban churches in China" with "an increasing number of urban intellectuals converting to Protestantism."[58] Many are beginning to call them "Chinese New Calvinists."[59] By 2019, a dozen of Timothy Keller's books had been translated and published in mainland China, making him the most influential brand of Calvinistic Christianity there.[60]

Since 2016, American journalist June Cheng wrote a series of stories for conservative evangelical media outlet *World* magazine on the Early Rain church in China. In her first story, titled "House Church on a Hill," Cheng refers to this ministry as "a trailblazing church" that is "launching political taboo initiatives and reshaping the face of the nation's house church movement."[61] For a few years, Cheng's reporting helped create a largely positive and even heroic image for this church leadership. Such publicity granted one of the founding pastors of this church, Wang Yi, a global celebrity status that China seldom churns out through its public media, which has always censored any mention of Christianity.

But as an ethnographic study shows, Early Rain's leadership had become influenced by YRR-style expansionism around 2013 and has since been plagued with manipulation, control, alleged sexual abuses, and cover-ups since 2014.[62] The church underwent a gradual theological change in emphasizing the spiritual authority of men over women. From 2012 to 2018,

---

56. Ma, *Religious Entrepreneurism*, 198.

57. Keller's ministry does use the word *brand* when referring to itself. For example, in a Redeemer City to City newsletter to invite year-end donations for its regional affiliates who "share our brand, our vision and mission, our ideology and philosophy." Keller, "Letter from Europe."

58. Cheng, "House Church on a Hill"; Chow, "Calvinist Public Theology."

59. Chow, "Calvinist Public Theology."

60. See book series in Chinese by Timothy Keller, https://book.douban.com/series/29237.

61. Cheng, "House Church on a Hill."

62. Ma, *Religious Entrepreneurism*, 211.

the exclusion of a founding female preacher was followed by the firing of a pregnant female teacher in the church school, and then multiple alleged sexual abuses. When the West was informed of this church's Conscience Prisoner ministry as a social justice program assisting families of Chinese dissidents, its director's alleged assaults on women were covered up by pastors. By the time these incidents were exposed and circulated on Chinese social media, this 700-member church had five alleged sexual predators. Most victims were single mothers and single women in the church community.

Despite the controversy, Western media has continued to look away and depicted these church leaders as practicing "civil disobedience" against a communist regime.[63] Articles published by The Gospel Coalition also boosted their fame among Reformed evangelicals in America.[64] Websites of the Ethics and Religious Liberty Commission of the SBC elevated this church leadership to modern day saints.[65]

In 2019, the celebrity pastor of this church Wang Yi launched a Jim Jones-style confrontation with the Chinese authorities, encouraging followers including young children to gather and pray in front of police stations for a prolonged time until some were arrested. On Chinese social media, Wang Yi described it as a "staged crash." Images of these "brave" Chinese Christians were then circulated overseas and picked up by Western media. Meanwhile, the appearance of a woman alleging sexual abuse twice brandishing a knife inside the church's sanctuary invited the intervention of local police but remained below the media radar. Two weeks later, the church was closed down. For his anti-communist communications, Wang Yi was arrested by the Chinese authorities. Both John Piper and Timothy Keller posted praising comments for this Chinese pastor on their social media accounts. The YRR movement platform The Gospel Coalition continued to publish a series of laudatory articles.[66]

When it comes to #MeToo, American journalists are known for their regular failures "to represent the reality and lived experiences of sexual violence" even in America.[67] Scholars point out that they are "not follow-

---

63. Metaxas, "China's Pastors Challenge Communist Govt."

64. Zylstra, "Young Restless, and Reformed in China"; Carter, "Persecuted Chinese Pastor"; Jun, "Five Lessons from Persecuted Christians."

65. Carter, "Five Facts about Persecuted Chinese Pastor"; Sobolik and Hough, "Increasing Religious Persecution in China."

66. Kidd, "China Sentences Pastor Wang Yi"; Zylstra, "How Chinese Pastors Developed Their Theology"

67. Royal, "Journalist Guidelines."

ing guidelines readily available to them and are therefore perpetuating inaccurate and damaging beliefs around the reality of sexual violence."[68] When it comes to events of seeming persecution in local movements of other countries, they habitually overlook the contextual facts of these happenings. What some scholars refers to as "communicative capitalism" in American electoral politics also applies to the media industry in general.[69] There is often an apparent gap between media discourses and the everyday complexities of reality. "The convergence of profit motives in media and discourse that generates a 'hyper-reality'[70] in which media professionals obscures, rather than analyzes or seeks to transform, the very condition of public ethics."[71]

In countries where Christianity continues to be in minority status and suffers political or cultural prejudice, the persecution narrative tends to become a dominant theme of journalistic work through Western media. The historical memory of severe persecution suffered by Christians in mainland China has been a convenient narrative for global media to overexploit. For example, in 2016, a church building in Henan province of China was demolished, killing the wife of a local pastor by accident. Western media reported this incident as an evidence of persecution and named the woman a "martyr."[72] But according to China mission expert Brent Fulton, the demolition happened because of "a land dispute . . . which happened to involve a pastor, his wife and their church."[73] In 2014, in an effort to mitigate the media's urge to portray every similar incident out of context, Fulton noted that "For every demolished church, one could point to thousands of others filled to capacity last Sunday with Christians who worshipped relatively unhindered."[74] For Christian media outlets or Christian reporters in this profession, and with the appeal to the consumers of American media, an "evangelical persecution syndrome" runs deep. Furthermore,

> [E]vangelicals saw the world [through] the lens of "victim identification." Over the past fifty years, American evangelicals became galvanized by a vision of their own (global) persecution. They

68. Royal, "Journalist Guidelines."
69. Dean, "Communicative Capitalism."
70. See Baudrillard, *Ecstasy of Communication*.
71. Salter, "Online Justice in the Circuit of Capital."
72. Chiaramonte, "Martyr Killed by Bulldozer."
73. Fulton, "Church in China Today."
74. Fulton, "Is There a Campaign against Christianity."

spoke of Christians being martyred all over the world, prevented from spreading the gospel and persecuted for their faith. These victims were sometimes American missionaries but more often were local Christian believers in Africa, Asia, or elsewhere who faced government oppression, conflict with other religious groups (often Muslims), or political marginalization. Evangelicals depicted these victims as facing persecution bravely, and consequently they became the role models. Believers in the United States were invited to see themselves as part of the global Christian family, and thus to identify with the victimization they saw elsewhere. By the turn of the twenty-first century, "persecution" had become a primary lens through which evangelicals viewed the world.[75]

Media professionals superficially engage in "a new form of evangelical internationalism,"[76] because "communist persecution of Christians became a primary lens through which American evangelicals thought about global politics."[77] McAlister wisely concludes that "Christian persecution, however real in certain times and places, also became a symbol that resonated far beyond what might be expected from the facts on the ground."[78] American journalists' work in other countries are more likely to be detached from reality due to lack of contextualized interactions and understanding. They have neither the local knowledge nor the incentive to avoid stereotypes. Even worse, they often turned out to be part of the problem. Their audiences often lack the sophistication to decipher a more nuanced story.

The Globalization of #MeToo

In 2018, the BBC reported that "the #MeToo movement sparked a debate about abuse in 85 countries, but it's not taken off in West Africa."[79] From 2017 to 2019, the #MeToo movement became a common language, a new liberation theology that united the oppressed around the globe.[80] One article in the *Telegraph* mapped a timeline with major spreading incidents in different continents of the world.

75. McAlister, *Kingdom of God*, 11.
76. McAlister, *Kingdom of God*, 2.
77. McAlister, *Kingdom of God*, 106.
78. McAlister, *Kingdom of God*, 289.
79. Ioussouf, "Why #MeToo."
80. Mahdavi, "How #MeToo."

As a viral campaign, part of the success of #MeToo has to do with how deeply personal it felt. Within days our social media feeds were flooded with friends and family members adding their stories. . . . In Spain it became #YoTambien, in France it became #BalanceTonPorc, roughly translated as "expose your pig"; in Italy #quellavoltache ("That Time When"). In Israel, a Hebrew phrase translated as "Us Too." In China, where Facebook is blocked, posts appeared briefly on local social media channels before being ripped down by censors.[81]

Australian journalist Tracey Spicer told the *Telegraph* that "globalization, connectivity and the women's rights movement have created the perfect storm."[82] She reckons that the internet and social media have changed everything, for "almost all of the whistleblowers . . . do so via Twitter (direct message) or Facebook (private message)." As *Foreign Policy* reports, "initial #MeToo accusations led to an avalanche of global resignations and oustings across the private and public sectors."[83] Despite the cultural, institutional, and legislative changes this movement brought so far, it has never been an easy battle for victims and advocates who got involved.

> To be sure, as the #MeToo movement achieves concrete victories, a backlash has also grown. Defamation suits, targeted harassment, and even arrests are all part of concerted efforts to disparage and silence women. There have been personal countersuits, as alleged perpetrators take their accusers to court for reputational damages. . . . [T]he fear is that the high cost of defending against these cases could scare off potential future victims from coming forward. . . . In other cases, governments have driven the backlash, with sinister consequences.[84]

In April of 2018, in the wake of #MeToo accusations against famous clergy on social media, Hong Kong Christian Council conducted a survey that revealed fifty-five reports of sexual abuses. A staff member told media that in the Chinese hierarchical structure of churches, "high-ranking" perpetrators easily prey on less powerful people "because they use the fact that they are widely trusted by the public."[85]

---

81. Burke, "#MeToo Shockwave."
82. Burke, "#MeToo Shockwave."
83. Stone and Vogelstein, "Celebrating #MeToo."
84. Stone and Vogelstein, "Celebrating #MeToo."
85. "#MeToo Complaints Rife in Hong Kong"; "Churches Need to Act."

In 2019, emboldened by the #MeToo movement in the US, celebrity photographer Busola Dakolo accused a famous pastor, Biodun Fatoyinbo, of rape by releasing a video post on social media, triggering Nigeria's #MeToo and #ChurchToo moment. The BBC describes Biodun Fatoyinbo as "a flamboyant pastor" who is the leading pastor of Nigeria's biggest and fastest growing church.[86] After the allegations went online, Pastor Fatoyinbo defended himself in an Instagram post but also decided to step down from his position.

Enabled by technology, Babel churches' and movements' urge for size, efficiency and other utilitarian results find renewed strength with global branding success. Decades ago, we entered the McDonaldization phase of Christianity. Anthropologists use the word "McDonaldization" to describe "the anodyne, sameness and packaged happiness promoted by global franchised businesses."[87] When this term is applied to the global spread of evangelical models, it overexploits the receiving community and exacerbates the problem. While in secular business, this means material exploitation, in the world of global Christianity, this leads to spiritual exploitation.

> [At] McDonalds . . . customers are being socialized to become part of the routinised world of service workers. Likewise, global televangelism is turning their audiences into their "labor force" as televangelists, such as Benny Hinn . . . ask for "co-laborers" (listeners) to financially support their global ministries. Through these ways, televangelism audiences are becoming socialized to the new "global church" built in virtual space.[88]

British sociologist Anthony Giddens's observes the consequences of the social changes marking the shift into "late modern" society: Modernity is marked by three primary structural changes: (1) the "disembedding" of social life in conjunction with a reliance on "abstract expert systems"; (2) the "institutionalization of reflexivity"; and (3) the process of globalization.[89] These levels of analysis help us grasp a nuanced understanding about globalization when "religious symbols, teachings and practices are easily 'disembedded,' that is, lifted out of one cultural setting, and

---

86. "Nigerian Pastor Biodun Fatoyinbo Steps Aside."
87. See Ritzer, *McDonaldization of Society*.
88. James, *McDonaldisation*, 7.
89. See Giddens, *Consequences of Modernity*, and *Modernity and Self-Identity*.

're-embedded' into another," according to sociologist Wade Clark Roof.[90] Another sociologist Lorne L. Dawson also writes,

> At the heart of the modern global social order is trust in the abstract systems of expertise that make our world work. It is these systems that guarantee a social and technological order to the relations between the local and the global, individuals and social systems, natur[e] and humanity. This trust is essential, yet it is imperiled by the very institutionalized reflexivity that warrants its existence in the first place. We are encouraged to question everything, even the expert systems. What is more, the modern societal need for trust happens in a new collective environment of risk unlike anything experienced by past societies.[91]

With mass media, the globalization of Christianity has the risk of becoming a cultural colonization project. Capital and brands now serve as the new colonizers of our day. To implant a brand into another context, there needs to be a dis-embedding process and a re-embedding process. Both chip off the essential personalism that is so central to the core message of the gospel. What is left with the brand is mainly religious symbolism and de-contextualized spirituality. Wade Clark Roof continues to describe:

> Given the extraction of symbols, teachings, and practices from their cultural origins and their instrumental use elsewhere, it is not surprising that questions are often raised about the authenticity and appropriateness of these new religious blendings, on the part particularly of indigenous peoples who sometimes feel "spiritually raped" in the process.... [I]t de-traditionalizes in the sense of fragmenting unities of experience, truth, and wisdom that took thousands of years to evolve. The binding power of religious traditions in providing meaning and identity is easily eroded: individuals feel less bound to a collective past or a shared present. Trust in others, so essential a foundation for personal identity, faith, and social relationships, becomes problematic.... [G]lobalization leads to mixed, often paradoxical, consequences. It creates a condition of living on the edge in a way that humanity has never lived before, yet at the same time creates possibilities for greater global solidarity.... [G]lobalization creates for people everywhere something of a perpetual liminal state—of being

---

90. Roof, *Spiritual Marketplace*, 73.
91. Dawson, *Comprehending Cults*, 57.

caught in between old ways of living and believing and the possibility of a new world in the making.[92]

In the economic realm, Americans have thought hard about the illusions of globalization. One of the defining scholarly works is *Globalization and Its Discontents*, by Nobel Prize laureate Joseph E. Stiglitz. The evangelical community has yet to formulate a spiritual understanding and response to the challenges of globalization. We ought to understand that the globalization of Christianity and the globalization of the marketplace happened simultaneously. And there is complexity to grasp with both the scattering and unity. As Walter Brueggemann says, we must "partake of the unity God wills and the scattering God envisions" because "any one-dimensional understanding of scattering denies God's vision for unity responsive to him. . . . [It] denies God's intent for the whole world as peopled by his many different peoples."[93] The gospel of Jesus Christ has deep personalism at its core. It is to be found in a real person-to-person community. The rationale of valuing the local church community is similar to that of buying local products. The local church ought to be the basic unit of personal and inter-personal expressions of the faith. Resisting impersonalism while cautiously making use of the conveniences of globalization may help us minimize its dark forces and maximize its benefits.

If we are not able to achieve this goal, we then over-rely on a mediated environment that becomes not only detached from place, but from time too. Consequently, the mediated environment creates multiple layers of alienation from reality. It is an artificial environment where spiritual deceptions thrive. In countries of the Global South, the theme of revivalism can be misused to generate such deceptions that are readily imbibed by the American audience. Or rather, Americans actually need them because "revivalism had been the constant refresher of American Protestantism—the smelling salts, rather than the opium of the masses."[94] They would like to think, after all, that God is working somewhere in the world, if not in secular America.

Through donations to foreign mission, unthinking embrace of the illusion of global evangelical revival amidst persecution, and wholesale use of mass media, American evangelicals have already participated in this global epidemic. Even the average American evangelical believer needs to

92. Roof, *Spiritual Marketplace*, 73–74.
93. Brueggemann, *Genesis*, 100–101.
94. Flake, *Redemptorama*, 30–31.

understand his or her endowed "privilege," which has implications for the spiritual well-being of many believers and unbelievers around the world.

At the receiving end of global mission, countries where Christianity just took root have no immunity or the ability to discern the toxic gene of Babel church. What meets the eyes of flesh seems to offer no hope. Consequently, we must return to the core message of Christianity—Jesus Christ.

Chapter 7

The Antidote: Philippians 2:5–8

Christ Jesus, who, being in very nature God, did not consider equality something to be used to his own advantage; rather, he made himself nothing by taking the very nature of a servant, being made in human likeness. And being found in appearance as a man, he humbled himself by becoming obedient to death—even death on a cross! —Philippians 2:5–8

The way of the Christian leader is not the way of upward mobility in which our world has invested so much, but the way of downward mobility ending on the cross. —Henri Nouwen

The rise and fall of Babel presents thought-provoking ironies. Babel builders' linguistic unity enabled them to launch an ambitious project, but that which aided their success also brought about the dissolution of that alliance. What they feared most about being scattered came to pass as a result of their own doing. Their architectural plan to reach the heavens was frustrated by God himself, who descended from heaven. The desire for fame was exchanged for a humiliating name "Babel" that would be a memorial to their folly. And in the end, it was their very action of gathering that led them to scatter and fill the earth. Walter Brueggemann points to the theme of irony as a hermeneutical key to this biblical text.

> When we notice the irony, we notice that the text speaks, perforce, in a double dialect. On the one hand, its language may be taken at face value by the innocent reader; on the other hand, what lies beneath the text contradicts the apparent meaning of a face-value reading. . . . It may well be that irony is the vehicle for traducing

the unsettled space between truth and power, for truth reading subverts power in the exposé of irony.¹

The same irony repeats itself in history. To publicly witness truth, the church needs to have visibility. But in order to protect and renew that authenticity, the church also needs to retreat to invisibility. Admittedly, this challenge to Christian mission is not unrelated to the paradoxical nature of the gospel itself. Take visibility for example. Jesus himself gave commands of public witness (Matt 5:14–15) as well as nondisclosure (Matt 8:4; Mark 7:36). If Jesus teaches Christians not to hide their light under a bushel, they ought to practice the faith with visibility. In fact, many believe that more visibility is better in a modern society that pushes religious faith to the private sphere. History offers abundant examples when Christian leadership rose to their public calling and served the wider society. German theologian Dietrich Bonhoeffer writes:

> The church-community has . . . a very real impact on the life of the world. It gains space for Christ. . . . All who belong to the body of Christ have been freed from and called out of the world. They must become visible to the world not only through the communal bond evident in the church-community's order and worship, but also through the new communal life among brothers and sisters in Christ.²

But at the same time, Jesus also warns about the danger of inauthenticity when believers practice their faith in public (Matt 6:5–6). There is a fine line between public witness and public fame. American evangelicalism is at a loss when it comes to Christians' suffering in obscurity. From its perspective, such suffering would mean futility, failure, and lack of influence. They are so success-minded that they have become entirely utilitarian, unappreciative of what is true self-denial.

Evangelicalism around the world can easily form an affinity with wealth, power, fame, and influence. Evangelical Christianity's moral ambiguity with entrepreneurial forces in the world began long before the crisis of modernity. However, as technological advances are shaping our culture in a more profound way, the impact of Babel church can be magnified. A free market society like America is an institutional environment that provides all the means—technology, mass media, consumerism,

---

1. Brueggemann, *Truth Speaks to Power*, 6-8.
2. Bonhoeffer, *Discipleship*.

global infrastructure, etc. Furthermore, utilitarian ethics direct evangelical Protestants to justify their use of these means by the end goal—of the sanctity of mission. Utilitarianism has blinded its ethical commitment. Reliance on mass media has distorted Babel churches' epistemology, their ability to know reality from illusion.

"Whatever Works": The Danger of Evangelical Ethics

The world hungers for God's spirit and revelation, but it also revolts against both. When we pray, "May your will be done on earth as it is in heaven," do we expect a change in ourselves? Often times, believers pray and hope that God will change the external environment. Our prayer can become a self-serving gibberish. The church has not been self-aware that it lives in a sphere of powers in their own right. Political power, wealth, the ability to control others, the self-will of moralism, are active spiritual forces, constantly demanding our allegiance. As scholars point out, despite the fact that evangelicals and their surrounding culture may seem antagonistic towards one another, they actually share four common traits: "a disinterest in tradition, a faith in technology, a drive toward popularization, and a belief in individualism."[3] Evangelicals driven by utilitarian ethics are ambivalent about the spiritual temptations of power in the public square. They assume that the church's task in society is to provide a moral basis for democratic order. This essentially Constantinian sentiment betrays a lust for political power.

With regard to the role of capital (e.g., ministry dollars), such utilitarian ethics also create a fundamental paradox for evangelicalism. "Being an evangelical means you want to spread the good word, but . . . in order to do this, you must reach beyond the walls of the church and into the secular marketplace."[4] During the competition against "the ever-growing array of more fun, more entertaining, and less guilt-ridden discretionary leisure time activities," churches and ministries unconsciously join the race to boost publicity and "match their message to the marketplace." Schuurman elaborates:

> Christian faith has undergone a shift: from a religiosity shaped by national boundaries and culture to a new situation shaped primarily by an open market. . . . [A]nd an open market becomes the primary reference point for Christian institutions, a sense of

3. Schultze, "Keeping the Faith."
4. Einstein, *Brands of Faith*, 65.

free choice and creative entrepreneurship replace the ethos of
citizenship, loyalty and obligation. This is the main exogenous
stimulus of social change that has allowed the creative and entertaining evangelical culture of the margins to shift closer to the
core of Christian activity in North America. Church attendance
is not culturally required anymore; and if it cannot be coercive,
it must become attractive. . . . The more intensive the human
management and control in a marketplace revival, often the
more grandiose the rhetoric against "formalism" or institutions
and the more daring the claim of divine presence and power. It
is an irony not many charismatic preachers would recognize, let
alone publicly acknowledge.[5]

American evangelicals' collective embrace of utilitarian ethics is a social learning process. Churches learn to create services based on consumer appeal, without realizing that they have allowed or embraced secularism. Religious entrepreneurs try to substitute structures of authority, predictability, and security for the unpredictable movement of God's spirit. Other sincere movement-makers are motivated by the same Constantinian impulse to dominate a culture with Christianity. In this way, such organizational changes are in fact political in nature. Losing authenticity and organic spontaneity from below, evangelical movements became ideology-making systems. "It is simply the nature of the dominant ideology of individualism shaped by the context of corporate capitalism."[6]

Thus, the gospel can be turned into propaganda. To Jacques Ellul, the definition of "propaganda" is not limited to the manipulation of public opinion in totalitarian regimes. In Western democracies such as the United States, he points out, "although there is no State or legal monopoly, there is, nevertheless, indeed a private monopoly."[7] According to Ellul, such is democratic propaganda:

> [W]hat happens as soon as the church avails itself of propaganda
> is a reduction of Christianity to the level of all other ideologies or
> secular religion. . . . Every time a church tried to act through the
> propaganda devices accepted by an epoch, the truth and authen-
> ticity of Christianity were debased. . . . Christianity . . . becomes
> institutionalized in all its expressions and compromised in all its
> actions. . . . [T]he church succeeds, just as all other organizations.

5. Schuurman, *Subversive Evangelical*, 161–62.
6. O'Neill, *Plato's Cave*, 52.
7. Ellul, *Propaganda*, 236.

It reaches the masses, influences collective opinions, leads sociological movements, and even makes many people accept what seems to be Christianity. But in doing that the church becomes a false church. It acquires power and influence that are of this world, and through them integrates itself into this world.[8]

Propaganda modes in democratic, capitalist countries lead to "psychological modifications" in the consciousness of the masses and consequently a mental universe foreign to truly authentic Christianity. It risks "the reduction of Christianity to the level of an ideology," which Jacques Ellul views as "the never-ending temptation held out to the church."[9]

> Day after day the wind blows away the pages of our calendars, our newspapers, and our political regimes, and we glide along the stream of time without any spiritual framework, without a memory, without a judgment, carried about by "all winds of doctrine" on the currents of history. . . . Now we ought to react vigorously against this slackness, this tendency to drift. If we are to live in this world, we need to know it far more profoundly; we need to rediscover the meaning of events, and the spiritual framework which our contemporaries have lost.[10]

To be sure, authentic Christianity ought not to be an ideology; rather, it should involve the doing-away with ideology. Nor should it be a religion as a way of pitting things that are sacred against those that are not. It is not a cultural artifact or even the basis for a static or highbrow culture. Authentic Christian faith is forming the whole person and the entirety of organic life into God's likeness as best revealed through Jesus Christ. As theologians Stanley Hauerwas and William H. Willimon put it, "The world was fundamentally changed in Jesus Christ, and we have been trying, but failing, to grasp the implications of that change ever since."[11]

"Even Death on the Cross": Jesus' #MeToo

There have been discussions about biblical themes related to #MeToo, including the often-mentioned stories of Dinah, Tamar, and Bathsheba.[12]

8. Ellul, *Propaganda*, 230.
9. Ellul, *Propaganda*, 231–32.
10. Ellul, *Presence of the Kingdom*, 138.
11. Hauerwas and Willimon, *Resident Aliens*, 17.
12. See Trible, *Texts of Terror*; Scott, "Bible's #MeToo Problems."

As author Ruth Everhart writes, "In what Phyllis Trible called its 'texts of terror,' the Bible tell harrowing tales of women being raped, sacrificed, and silenced by members of their own family. . . . Their stories can be . . . warnings about what happens when the powerful become corrupt and the vulnerable are silenced."[13] The Bible invites its readers to note these women. But we might still ask: Does God give us any mandate about how to respond to these horrific incidents? If so, how do these mandates help us arrive at a public theology in response to today's #MeToo and #Church-Too movements? In this section, I choose to look at two different passages in the Bible, Philippians 2:6–11 and Judges 19, which are not commonly interpreted as #MeToo narratives. Nevertheless, they are helpful in unveiling some biblical mandates for the Christian community when it comes to such traumatizing experiences.

German theologian Jürgen Moltmann writes in *The Crucified God*, "In Christianity the cross is the test of everything which deserves to be called Christian."[14] Apart from the Gospels, Philippians 2:6–11 serves as the best text to drive home this core message. This christological hymn reveals the dramatic distance Jesus traveled from the "form of God" to "the death on the cross." It presents a movement contrasting with the narrative of Babel in Genesis 11:1–9. As Babel went upward, Christ chose downward mobility. Babel looked impressive to human eyes, but Christ had no grandeur to present. Babel built itself up, but Christ emptied himself. Fourteenth-century Orthodox theologian Nicholas Cabasilas wrote in *The Life in Christ* about the divine virtue of "coming down."

> Just as human affection, when it abounds, overpowers those who love and causes them to be beside themselves, so God's love for men emptied God. He does not stay in His own place and call the slave; He seeks him in person by coming down to him. He who is rich reaches the pauper's hovel, and He displays His love by approaching in person. He seeks love in return and does not withdraw when he is treated with disdain. He is not angry over ill treatment, but He sits by the door and does everything to show us that He loves, even enduring suffering and death to prove it.[15]

The core message of Christianity is about a God who traveled an impossible distance by bending down towards humanity. Evangelical author

13. Everhart, "Women of the Bible Say #MeToo."
14. Moltmann, *Crucified God*, 1.
15. Cabasilas, *Life in Christ*, 644–45, 162–63.

and #MeToo advocate Mary DeMuth also refers to these accommodating acts as God's own "Me Too moment": "Almighty God slipped into the skin of a baby. . . . to live life alongside us, walk dusty pathways, grieve loss, experience betrayal, watch sunsets, harbor disappointments, and be abused. . . . [W]hatever trials or temptations or despairs we face, he can always say, 'Me too.'"[16]

At the end of the downward movement showing God's cascading love for humanity is a naked Jesus of Nazareth. Philippians 2:5–11 strenuously brings this visual shock to us by the verse "even death on the cross." The humiliating aspect of the crucifixion includes nudity and exposure of the person's private parts. In a word, the death of Jesus on a cross was a gruesome scene.

Some scholars raise the question of whether Jesus was in fact a victim of sexual abuse.[17] African American scholar Wil Gafney finds it necessary to "consider anew the full range of torture and humiliation to which Jesus of Nazareth was subjected, physical and sexual."[18] He affirms that "the latter is so traumatizing for the Church that we have covered it up—literally—covering Jesus's genitals on our crucifixes."[19] As American theologian Elaine Heath writes, "In Jesus's culture, as in Middle Eastern cultures today, to be stripped naked in front of a watching crowd was an act of sexual violation. . . . The torture was sadistic, carried out while he was naked in order to maximize his humiliation in front of the voyeuristic crowd."[20] Australian Catholic scholar Michael Trainor also agrees on the basis of textual evidence: "Ancient texts outside the Second Testament can also help us get a sense of what crucifixion would mean in the Greco-Roman, Jewish world, particularly as a heinous form of public punishment, designed to expose its victim to the utmost public ridicule, shame, and abuse."[21] He reckons that the crucifixion is "in a powerful and public way . . . an act of sexual abuse."[22]

> The soldiers' act of stripping Jesus has two intentions: to shame him publicly and to eliminate his identity represented through his own clothing. The act changes his identity and makes him

16. DeMuth, *We Too*, 162.
17. See Heath, *Healing the Wounds of Sexual Abuse*, and *We Were the Least of These*.
18. Gafney, "Crucifixion and Sexual Violence."
19. Gafney, "Crucifixion and Sexual Violence."
20. Heath, *We Were the Least of These*, 123.
21. Trainor, "Mark's Passion Narrative."
22. Trainor, "Mark's Passion Narrative."

naked.... They intend to make him the object of disgrace and grotesquery. The scene thus becomes a highpoint of abuse second only to his public execution.... Symbolically, Matthew's Jesus is not only subject to physical abuse, falsely accused and condemned by the machinations of political and religious officialdom. He is now subject to sexual abuse. The exposure of his penis, the symbol of sexual power and identity, is the ultimate act of shaming and abuse. The forced removal of his clothes erases his social identity. He is now without any cultural, social, religious, political and sexual status.[23]

American evangelical author Jayme R. Reaves proposes that "the stigma and expected loss of respect" might be reasons why the claim that Jesus was a victim of sexual abuse is often resisted or ignored in the Christian circle, for fear that it would "lower Jesus in the eyes of decent people."[24] She adds that this reaction is often an instinctive response rather than a conscious one. Pushing the argument further, she relates Jesus' experience to the way churches respond to the #MeToo movement:

> Jesus' experience of sexual abuse carries extraordinary potential for significant change within the churches on how sexual violence might be seen and how the needs of survivors should be addressed. The naming of Jesus as a victim challenges churches to rethink misplaced attitudes that contribute to blaming, stigmatization, and shaming.... The issues highlighted by #MeToo, #ChurchToo, #SilenceIsNotSpiritual, and church sexual abuse scandals, thereby offer a belated opportunity for transformative renewal within theology, and within the church.[25]

There are also other Bible passages that echo Jesus' solidarity with victims of sexual abuse. In their important book *Geography of Grace*, Kris Rocke and Joel Van Dyke begin with an unusual exegesis of Judges 19, arguably the most gruesome story in the Bible next to Jesus' crucifixion. It tells how a nameless concubine of a Levite was gang-raped, savagely beaten, then murdered by dismemberment at the hands of the Levite. What followed was another civil war in which 600 more women were turned into sex slaves. Rocke and Van Dyke ponder what kind of grace may come out of the tale of this nameless and voiceless Levite concubine, the victim of horrifying sexual

---

23. Trainor, *Body of Jesus and Sexual Abuse*, 147–48.
24. Reaves, "#MeToo Jesus."
25. Reaves, "#MeToo Jesus."

THE ANTIDOTE: PHILIPPIANS 2:5–8

abuse. "Where is God for the unnamed woman?" they ask.[26] They reflect on how "grace flows downhill and pools up in Judges 19."[27]

> Is it possible that God is really Immanuel to an unnamed sex slave that is gang-raped and dismembered? If we reflect long enough and look deeply into her heart, we discover the unthinkable. Or to be more precise, we are discovered by it. . . . As it turns out, this unnamed woman was born in an insignificant town called Bethlehem. This key, mentioned no less than four times, turns and liberates our imagination. Jesus was not only born in Bethlehem, but on the night that he was betrayed and abandoned into the hands of his enemies, he broke the bread, which was his body, and gave it to the twelve disciples. . . . If we reflect long enough on the heart of the unnamed woman, we will come to know not only her heart, but her name as well. . . . [S]he teaches us a hard but liberating truth—that she was not alone in her abandonment. She was not alone when she was handed over to the mob. She was not along when she was gang-raped and beaten that night. She alone was not cut into twelve pieces and handed out to Israel. God was with her that night. God too was abused, beaten, raped, and dismembered. Where is God? God is with us, particularly the least. Immanuel.[28]

Many advocates and biblical scholars affirm that Scripture itself gives voice to the voiceless and declares God's solidarity with the victim. God is the God of the voiceless, the nameless, the marginalized and the abused within and without the religious community. In situations of controversy, Jesus himself identified with the condemned and the shameful ones. Often these were women. Through the words of Lady Wisdom in the book of Proverbs, God also has a female voice. These days God has raised her voice through the #MeToo and #ChurchToo movements. The abuse of power, cover-ups and protectionism are not news to God. *Geography of Grace* also associates this with the #MeToo moment of Jesus' own physical nakedness:

> Jesus never allowed fear for his reputation (in any conventional sense) to guide his steps. He occupies all of the insulting epithets hurled at him with surprisingly little concern. He barely acknowledges his accusers, let alone defends himself against them. His interests lie elsewhere. He allows himself to be so thoroughly associated with the shameful ones as to be one of them. . . . While Jesus is

26. Rocke and Van Dyke, *Geography of Grace*, 39.
27. Rocke and Van Dyke, *Geography of Grace*, 42.
28. Rocke and Van Dyke, *Geography of Grace*, 42–43.

naked and exposed to the world, he calls things what they are, while simultaneously clothing with forgiveness that which he exposes.[29]

The example of Jesus Christ remains a revolutionary one to every age because it springs from a fundamentally different kind of life than what the world knows. Organic life has spontaneity at its core. A spontaneous movement begins with our imitation of Christ, including dying to our self, and the mortification of our infatuation with speed and size.

A primary mandate from the #MeToo movement to the public might be "listen to the women." Additional discussions center around the power dynamics in workplace, social life, and faith communities. But within evangelical churches, even these lessons are taking a long time to set in. Silence and denials are overwhelmingly the norm. The church has not been ready to embrace either the biblical revelation or popular mandates that have reshaped societal norms. Former prosecutor Bob Tchvidijian told media how he realized the evangelical failure by protecting the powerful when he handled thousands of abuse cases in the 1990s: "Many church leaders and church members had no problem coming to court and testifying on behalf of the character of the defendant . . . few came in defense of the victim."[30] He observed this happening in about nine of ten cases. He was appalled. "There's something wrong with that. The Jesus I know was always on the side of the wounded and the marginalized." This became a career-changing moment for Tchvidijian to start GRACE (Godly Response to Abuse in the Christian Environment) in 2003.

After the #MeToo movement, there has been scant public theology development on the topic, except for the article previously quoted from the *International Journal of Public Theology*.[31] It laid the foundation for public theologians to re-engage with the #MeToo movement. By interpreting the silence of God in Philippians 2 and Judges 19 as not divine inaction, we may be able to derive a few mandates. First, God himself identifies with victims of sexual abuse because he has been there. This is why many advocates say that God is speaking through #MeToo victims. This part of God's speech needs to be recognized. After all, doesn't the cross teach us that God speaks from his own vulnerability?

Second, public exposure of how such abuses happened is mandatory. Doing so not only unveils the darkness but cautions against further harm

29. Rocke and Van Dyke, *Geography of Grace*, 186, 197.
30. Bruinius, "Churches Struggle."
31. Reaves, "#MeToo Jesus."

by the same sexual predators in the community. On an intuitive level, most victims of such abuses feel the need of open communication within a faith community. It offers an opportunity for the church to become a listening and mourning communion. As Ruth Everhart puts it, "One of the challenges facing today's church is the need to respond to the ongoing revelations that women have been sexually victimized by men for far too long."[32] This also means that whoever exposes the abuses is justified in doing so. In fact, these advocates (sometimes victims themselves) become part of God's ongoing speech through this trauma. Trying to silence or bring retaliation against these individuals is an action against God.

Third, how church leaders react to #MeToo is a moment that tests their authenticity. Sadly, real life scenarios show us that the manipulative post-abuse response from evangelicals can be equally, if not more, traumatizing to victims than the actual abuses. If leaders choose silencing and denial, based on the previous two mandates, then the worst fruits of spiritual corruption ought to unveil what went wrong systematically with their ministry. The more "influential" or famous this ministry is, the more toxic its culture may have become. If this moment of truth brings leaders to humility and true repentance, then the scandal may lead to genuine healing and spiritual growth. In any case, the #MeToo movement mandates that Christian communities offer a "public lamentation."[33]

Resisting Babel

Babel proclaimed ambition, but Christ spoke brokenness. Babel exploited resources out of self-serving lust, but Christ did not seek his own advantage. Babel created an illusion, but Christ ushered in an ultimate reality. Thomas Merton once claimed, "There is no greater disaster in the spiritual life than to be immersed in unreality, for life is maintained and nourished in us by our vital relation with realities outside and above us. When our life feeds on unreality, it must starve."[34] He reaffirms the subtlety of this spiritual danger:

> In Jesus we meet not a presentation of basic ideas about God, world, and humanity, but an invitation to join up, to become part of a movement, a people. By the very act of our modern theological attempts at translation, we have unconsciously distorted the

32. Everhart, *#MeToo Reckoning*, 233.
33. Everhart, *#MeToo Reckoning*, 209.
34. Merton, *Thoughts in Solitude*, 3.

gospel and transformed it into something it never claimed to be—
ideas abstracted from Jesus, rather than Jesus with his people.[35]

Over the history of missions, the Babel rhetoric of movement-building has almost always failed. At the beginning of the twentieth century, world evangelist John R. Mott promoted the slogan of "the evangelization of the world in this generation." Yet, a century has passed, and the world is in a situation closer to the saying of Jesus, "When the son of man comes, will he find faith on the earth?" Os Guinness points out that "the problem is not that Christians have disappeared, but that Christian faith has become so deformed. Under the influence of modernity, we modern Christians are literally capable of winning the world while losing our own souls."[36] Protestantism's symbiotic relationship with modernity is manifested within trends of American and global evangelicalism. Rather than maintaining its own integrity, Protestant evangelicalism has repeatedly danced to the latter's changing rhythms. As Martin Marty puts it, "Evangelicalism is the characteristic Protestant way of relating to modernity."[37]

The biblical message of the gospel of Jesus Christ contains ultimate truth claims. Christianity offers a God-centered worldview with certainty. But paradoxically, in real life, our fallen and messy human condition is much more complicated than textbooks. We do not live a robotic existence, and no single remedy can quickly snap away the fallen condition. Real life is organic, and a fallen real life can be painfully slow in recovery, even to when exposed to correct theological truths. Moreover, spiritual temptations are complicated too. What good and evil look like in real life are more nuanced than black and white. That is why these temptations are hard to detect. If we always live in a haste to accomplish things, we tend to be blind towards the spiritual temptations in day-to-day life. Because efficiency is a cultural demand, Christians need to return to a "liturgy of the ordinary," as described by Anglican priest Tish Harrison Warren:

> In a culture that craves the big, the entertaining, the dramatic, and the shocking (sometimes literally), cultivating a life with space for silence and repetition is necessary for sustaining a life of faith. . . . Repentance is not usually a moment wrought in high

---

35. Merton, *Thoughts in Solitude*, 21.
36. Guinness, *Dining with the Devil*, 43.
37. Marty, "Revival of Evangelicalism."

THE ANTIDOTE: PHILIPPIANS 2:5-8

drama. It is the steady drumbeat of a life in Christ and, therefore, a day in Christ.[38]

Discerning good from evil in the happenings of everyday life is a human struggle. But this slow pace-setting mentality sets the tone for all subsequent formation. The foundation of leadership integrity is paying attention to the "habits of the heart." It is part of knowing oneself with honesty. The antidote to Babel church is simply Christ-like character with humility and honesty at its core. Such character formation comes from a few spiritual disciplines, such as genuine confession, self-denial, and neighborliness.

Confession unto repentance and contemplation ought to be the church's definitive activities. As Jennifer McBride writes based on Dietrich Bonhoeffer's *Ethics* that "responsible repentance" ought to be a constant attitude of true believers, for Bonhoeffer argues, "everyone who acts responsibly by living according to Christ-reality becomes guilty."[39] He adds,

> [T]he church not only confesses sin but also opens itself up to further guilt through responsible repentance. Even if it discerns wisely, the church that risks attempts at transformative action within life's ethical complexities will become guilty to some degree, because, limited by its creatureliness, the church cannot ever enact perfect justice and healing.[40]

In church history, Augustine of Hippo (354–430 AD) probably was the exemplar prodigal who lived out this lesson. Trained in rhetoric to be a powerful and persuasive orator, young Augustine enjoyed public prestige. Struggling with lust and sexual temptations, the then-Manichaean believer Augustine nevertheless lived a double life. In 384 AD, Augustine moved to Milan to seek new opportunities and success but was influenced by Ambrose, who defended the Old Testament against Manichaean criticisms. Next came a well-known moment of his conversion when Augustine heard the voice of a child from a house nearby, urging him to read the Bible. The providential reading of Romans 13:13–14 cleansed his soul, and Augustine left the career of rhetorician and teacher to become a contemplative theologian.

---

38. Warren, *Liturgy of the Ordinary*, 33, 57.
39. Cited in McBride, *Church for the World*, 140–41.
40. Cited in McBride, *Church for the World*, 140–41.

Years later, Augustine offered mature insights on the danger of vainglory, the opposite of self-denial. In distinguishing between the city of God and the city of this world, Augustine wrote:

> Accordingly, two cities have been formed by two loves: the earthly city by the love of self, even to the contempt of God; the heavenly by the love of God, even to the contempt of self. The former, in a word, glories in itself; the latter in the Lord. For the one seeks glory from [human beings]; but the greatest glory of the other is God, the witness of conscience. The one lifts up its head in its own glory; the other says to its God: "You are my glory, and the lifter of my head."[41]

The discipline of self-denial through deep reflection and contemplation also applies to the way Christians conduct life together. It helps people to distinguish between the way gifts of charisma are seen as a creation-affirming and how such gifts are misused to equal prideful accomplishment. The latter is also known as "vainglory."

Vainglory leads one into self-deception through three typical practices: boasting, hypocrisy, and presumption of novelties.[42] The first two are common categories that are easy to understand. The last one refers to "using, having, or doing the latest and greatest, new and improved, unique and original thing to produce amazement in one's audience and thereby attract (positive) attention to oneself."[43] These common behavioral patterns all require an audience. Therefore, vainglory comes hand in hand with impression management. The reason vainglory has been considered in church traditions as one of the deadliest vices is that it leads to "dispositional patterns of thought, feeling, and behavior, not individual actions."[44] In other words, vainglory is deadly to the soul because it tends to "warp our character over a lifetime."[45] An initial genuine desire to help others and to achieve something for the God may gradually be transformed into a drive to manipulate for self-serving purposes. Self-denial is a journey turning away from our narcissistic tendencies and toward finding our true self in God. As Chuck DeGroat writes, "Dismantling the narcissistic false self is an act of dying—dying to illusion, to control, and

---

41. Augustine, *City of God*, Book XIV.28.
42. See DeYoung, *Vainglory*.
43. DeYoung, *Vainglory*, 37–38.
44. DeYoung, *Vainglory*, 37.
45. DeYoung, *Vainglory*, 37.

to fear. And it's also an act of resurrection—to truth, to vulnerability, to creativity, and to connection."[46]

Churches today are in dire need of humble and neighborly leadership. American psychologist David J. Ward writes that in religious contexts, "healthy spiritual leadership respects individual autonomy, tolerates and encourages critical thinking, and is appreciative of any power inequality."[47] Because of the power differential between a religious leader and a lay believer, and also because the latter often approaches in times of vulnerability, a religious leader needs to show genuine respect, usually by listening and compassionate advice. One role model of such leadership is Fred Rogers, a contemporary of the most infamous televangelists of 1980s, who used the same mass media technique innovatively and authentically. After having watched some distasteful TV program on the family's first television set in the 1950s, Fred Rogers learned two things. First, he found the children's programming destructive, with people throwing pies at each other. Second, he had an intuition that television had great potential for something extraordinarily good. Rogers recognized a particular trait of this mass media technique: "It's very, very personal, this medium."[48] He took great care not to abuse this given intimacy and trust:

> As he said no to greater speed, more money, and higher ratings, he said yes to quieter goods; thoughtfulness, intentionality, and his own intuition and imagination for the work, those very same values that pointed him, that second life-changing Easter, toward television as a force for greater good . . .[49]

Creativity needs to be checked by faithfulness. Our creativity should not manifest developments that thwart God's divine will for human flourishing. It ought to be used with care. As Rogers's biographer writes, "In the space between his gaze and the gaze of each child watching, he created an intimate world of safety and calm."[50] Even after gaining enormous fame, Fred Rogers practiced humility and acted against vainglory:

> Fred felt great ambivalence about fame. . . . His good friend Christopher de Vinck recalled that Fred would share his high-profile

---

46. DeGroat, *When Narcissism Comes to Church*, 11.
47. Ward, "Lived Experience of Spiritual Abuse."
48. Quoted in Tuttle, *Exactly as You Are*, 41.
49. Tuttle, *Exactly as You Are*, 36.
50. Tuttle, *Exactly as You Are*, 13.

appearances and greatest honors only obliquely. "I'm going to go to California to do a little TV work," he might say when he was going to appear on *The Tonight Show*, or "Joanne and I are going to spend a few days in Washington, DC," when he was going to receive the Presidential Medal of Freedom. From the very beginning, since working for the stars on the NBC sets in New York, Fred Rogers said no to the entitlements of fame.[51]

A more recent example is evangelical pastor Francis Chan, who, after realizing the tempting nature of fame, made a voluntary retreat from his celebrity status as a megachurch founder to a more obscure position.[52] A humbled ego obtains spiritual sensitivity to any move of the narcissistic self. It searches for the "True Self" and for God's work in day to day circumstances without abstracting theology about God. Franciscan priest Richard Rohr writes concerning the "True Self" forming a communion with Christ himself:

> The True Self has already overcome the contradictions and paradoxes of life, which is symbolized by the Risen Christ who presents the full tension of death and life, earth and spirit, human and divine—and precisely as overcome. That is the standing message that the Resurrected One holds for all of history. He holds and overcomes the ultimate and major tensions of humanity. In one glorious body, he unites our highest aspirations with the very deepest flesh of our being—which heals everything.[53]

Spiritual health of the soul comes from self-denial, leading to the rediscovery of one's true self. Theologian Stanley Hauerwas suggests that Christians should grow into a statue of self-denial, which can grant them beneficial "moments of self-forgetfulness."[54] The road of recovery for egoism lies in the truth of Matthew 16:25: "whoever wants to save their life will lose it, but whoever loses their life for me will find it" (NIV). The next verse shows that Jesus considers the word "life" to be synonymous here with here "soul." ("What good will it be for someone to gain the whole world, yet forfeit their soul?")

---

51. Tuttle, *Exactly as You Are*, 39.
52. Chan, *Letters to the Church*. I thank Casey Jen for this reminder.
53. Rohr, *Immortal Diamond*, 48.
54. Hauerwas, *Christian Existence Today*, 50.

THE ANTIDOTE: PHILIPPIANS 2:5–8

Slow Kingdom, Good Power

In conclusion, we might ask: What happened after Babel? And what can be done about today's Babel churches? To the first question, theologian Stanley Hauerwas points to humanity's relearning of a kind of "humility that ennobles."[55] Even God's act of confusing people's languages and his scattering of them was meant as a gift. After being divided and having to face the "otherness" as a result of linguistic and geographical differences, human beings were constantly reminded of their creaturely status. We need to seek the common speech of Christ in order to grow again into a healthy unity without fear and coercion.

Today, when religious entrepreneurs claim to want "Christian influence" or "public witness for the gospel," what they truly desire is a worldly kind of power. With power at its core, Babel church is a Constantinian project. Stanley Hauerwas describes such power-obsession: "Not content to wait, in time we try to make God's unity a reality for all people through coercion rather than witness."[56] Instead of showing the world what it means to be a community of humility through repentance, Babel Christianity seeks to make the world into a kingdom of power and fame.

In a book titled *Slow Church*, one of the co-authors, John Pattison, describes his frustrations at seeing how his own local church tried to replicate Willow Creek in the late 1990s. Pattison later affirms that "Jesus' description of the kingdom of God as being like yeast and a mustard seed imply a framework for growth that is organic, often invisible to the naked eye and ultimately mysterious."[57] They happen in the mundane parts of everyday life as well as unprecedented crises. In a culture that tempts us to speed up, "we are bound to each other" by commitment. Regarding the kingdom, he says: "It is a way of crafting a new, shared story for the community, while connecting us to the cosmic church across time and prefiguring the kingdom of God."[58]

This reflection on Babel churches also leads us to delve into a theology of power in general. In today's "I can" society, power takes a myriad of unfettered, aggressive forms. It engulfs all areas—politics, business, law, higher education, etc. What is God's response to this real abuse of power?

55. Hauerwas, *Christian Existence Today*, 49.
56. Hauerwas, *Christian Existence Today*, 53.
57. Smith and Pattison, *Slow Church*, 41.
58. Smith and Pattison, *Slow Church*, 43.

In the Bible, there is a passage where God's contempt for the abuse of power is plainly evident—the encounter between Jesus and Pilate. The silence of Jesus before Pilate shows that when truth confronts power, the latter flouts truth in the face, revealing its own fraudulence. Another example is a Pharisee's kind of piety, a power that was theologically charged. But when these figurees adopted a speech of religious power, God spoke a different speech—Christ.

Authentic Christianity holds the key narrative of a good kind of power by way of Christ's incarnation, crucifixion, and resurrection. Jesus not only survived the trauma of abuse, but death itself. His good, meek, and life-transforming power is a common speech that unites us all. It restores the chaos after Babel. The challenge is how to retain a strong prophetic voice for the world without that voice betraying the particular Christ-speech about God. Walter Brueggemann refers to it as "a subversion of reality" according to "a different way of imagining." To give fuller context, he calls us to:

> get up and utter a subversion of reality, an alternative version of reality that says another way of life in the world is not only possible but is peculiarly mandated and peculiarly valid. It is a subversion because we must fly low, stay under the radar, and hope not to be detected too soon, a subversion because it does indeed intend to subvert the dominant version of and to empower a community of subversives who are determined to practice their lives according to a different way of imagining.[59]

We need to be grounded in a reality that in the malfeasance we see in this world, from regime to church, there is a kind of power that is good. God rules from the power of Jesus Christ's crucifixion and resurrection. And because he discerns good from evil with absolute clarity and integrity, that good power cannot be abused. In the mission field of trauma, it flows with profound healing power into the lives of the most vulnerable. Even in the midst of America and the world's media cacophony around the #MeToo and #ChurchToo movements, that good power rules by shining a piercing light on the hard realities. Nothing can separate true believers from the love of God, not even a distorted Christianity. And that should be good news for us all.

---

59. Brueggemann, *Deep Memory*, 5.

Epilogue

Why does a researcher of mainland Chinese origin write a book about the pitfalls of American evangelicalism? Since this book germinated from a conversation I had with an American missionary to China, I will end it by bringing missions to China back into the conversation.

In the latter half of the nineteenth century, after the Second Opium War (1856–1860), an imperial China reluctantly allowed Western missionaries to enter through its treaty ports. Among an increasing number of women missionaries from America was Katharine Bushnell, who set sail for China in 1879.[1] Like many others, Bushnell desired to "bring the advantages of Christianity to women in foreign lands."[2]

But a few years later, this missionary woman's personal trajectory took a dramatic turn that differentiated her from most other mission workers. While serving in Singapore and Hong Kong, Bushnell found herself faced with an appalling system of public prostitution set up by Western male missionaries. She further investigated the matter and concluded that this sex trade was entirely "the product of Western civilization." Although East Asian countries had prostitutes, it was never before an organized industry. In her own words, such systemic abuse of women were "utterly unknown in China except in the treaty ports" where Westerners were concentrated.[3] After uncovering the involvement of male missionaries in setting up these public prostitution institutions, Bushnell attributed it to "the culpability of *Christian* men" in a report.[4] She pointed

1. Bushnell, *Dr. Katharine C. Bushnell*.
2. Du Mez, *New Gospel for Women*, 27.
3. Andrew and Bushnell, *Heathen Slaves and Christian Rulers*, quoted in Du Mez, *New Gospel for Women*, 79.
4. Du Mez, *New Gospel for Women*, 79.

out that "it was the influence of Western Christian 'civilization' that exploited Chinese practices and fashioned the system of sexual slavery that had taken hold wherever the two cultures intermingled."[5]

Discovering Western missionary misconduct in China became a turning point for Katharine Bushnell toward advocacy for indigenous women. Personally, I had a revelation similar to that of Katharine Bushnell. In the course of more than a decade of research on China's growing Protestant population, I have published on the growth, movements, and potential problems inside the Chinese church.[6] In particular, I have documented the historical context and events of an internationally known church community that had received the widest Western media publicity. Under an increasingly authoritarian Chinese regime, its pastors and ministry leaders became tokenized Christian heroes for religious freedom by Western media. Since 2010, this church leadership collaborated with missionaries from two conservative Reformed denominations in America. The ministry began to expand while internal controversies worsened.

In 2019, I published a book titled *Religious Entrepreneurism in China's Urban Churches: The Rise and Fall of Early Rain Presbyterian Reformed Church*. It uncovers another side of the story, including a range of power abuses in the church starting around 2013. Most Western media looked away from these red flags when the church has drifted from its "city on the hill" mission. The worst cases were alleged sexual abuses of single women and single mothers by multiple predators.

After the book's release, for more than a year, I faced both pushback and verbal attacks that most #MeToo advocates have typically experienced. A China mission organization (which I quoted from public sources in the book) and its so-called "missionaries" retaliated. Male colleagues within my field wrote lambasting reviews of the book.[7] One of the alleged abusers continued to harass a victim/survivor. I had to navigate these harsh realities just as Katharine Bushnell stubbornly plowed through resistance from her China mission board.

But until this day, Western media has perpetuated the success story of this flagship congregation such that no media wanted to turn the narrative around. Why would they? There is no accountability for the few American

---

5. Du Mez, *New Gospel for Women*, 83.

6. See Ma and Li, *Surviving the State, Remaking the Church* and Ma, *Chinese Exodus*.

7. For example, Doyle, "Missed Opportunity." Vala, "Book Review: Religious Entrepreneurism."

journalists and organizations carrying the narrative, if doing so only damages a number of alleged #MeToo victims in faraway China. And during increasing political antagonism between the US and China through a trade war and later a pandemic, who would want another anti-communist Christian hero to fall from grace?

But to me, on a personal level, this situation has been awfully wrong. In post-reform China, where evangelical Christianity presents a new source of hope, I saw the potential dangers of a Babel church model, assisted by mass media and an emerging celebrity evangelical culture, all exported from America. New converts in China had no prior knowledge about what might be the problematic brands of evangelicalism. There is no independent media in China to expose power abuses within the church. Quite the contrary, within the marginalized subculture of evangelical Chinese churches, there has been a strong motivation to protect the reputation of church leaders. These factors have collectively produced a fertile soil for abuse of power by church leadership.

Meanwhile, outside of China, Western media tends to over-politicize Christian growth in China as a democratizing process. It is also prone to tokenize and aggrandize celebrity Chinese pastors to the American public. Together, these multiple levels of irresponsibility contributed to evangelical Protestantism's loss of respectability and credibility among the average Chinese. Consequently, the rapid growth of churches since the early 1990s had visibly plateaued by 2020.

Similar things are happening in other regions where America is sending missionaries. What history taught Katharine Bushnell, tragically, continues to repeat itself in other parts of the world. Let's face it. Evangelical Protestantism is an invasive species. With globalization, it has aggressively expanded to the rest the world while failing to fix its own dysfunctions. How do we proceed from here? This book is not meant to provide all the answers. If anything, my hope is that it may be a catalyst for important conversations about what fruits we as the global body of Christ, through our response to the #MeToo and #ChurchToo movements, may bring to the world.

Bibliography

Abu-Nasr, D. "Promise Keepers Seek Global Presence." *The Austin-American Statesman*, October 6, 1997.
"Al Mohler Is Apologizing for Supporting Former Sovereign Grace Leader C. J. Mahaney." *Relevant*, February 15, 2019. https://relevantmagazine.com/current/al-mohler-is-apologizing-for-supporting-former-sovereign-grace-leader-c-j-mahaney/.
Allen, Bob. "Abuse Survivors Want Conference Speaker Removed." *Baptist News Global*, September 10, 2015.
Andrew, Elizabeth, and Katharine Bushnell. *Heathen Slaves and Christian Rulers*. Salt Lake City: Project Gutenberg, 2004.
Andrews, Matt. "What's Wrong with the Promise Keepers." *Midwest Today*, April/May, 1996. http://www.midtod.com/9603/promise.phtml.
Applebome, Peter. "Bakker Is Convicted on All Counts: First Felon among TV Evangelists." *The New York Times*, October 6, 1989.
Asamoah-Gyah, J. K. "Anointing through the Screen: Neo Pentecostalism and Televised Christianity in Ghana." *Studies in World Christianity* 11 (2005) 1.
Asghar, Rob. "Mars Hill: Cautionary Tale from the Enron of American Churches." *Forbes* September 16, 2014. https://www.forbes.com/sites/robasghar/2014/09/16/mars-hill-cautionary-tales-from-the-enron-of-american-churches/.
Augustine. *The City of God*. Hyde Park, NY: New City, 2012.
Bailey, Susan Pulliam. "Evangelical Leaders Stand by Pastor Accused of Abuse Cover-up." *Religion News Service*, May 24, 2013.
———. "In an Age of Trump and Stormy Daniels, Evangelical Leaders Face Sex Sandals of Their Own." *The Washington Post*, March 30, 2018. https://www.washingtonpost.com/news/acts-of-faith/wp/2018/03/30/in-an-age-of-trump-and-stormy-daniels-evangelical-leaders-face-sex-scandals-of-their-own/.
———. "Megachurch Pastor Bill Hybels Resigns from Willow Creek after Women Allege Misconduct." *The Washington Post*, April 11, 2018. https://www.washingtonpost.com/news/acts-of-faith/wp/2018/04/10/bill-hybels-prominent-megachurch-pastor-resigns-from-willow-creek-following-allegations/.
———. "Megachurch Pastors Leave Reformed Evangelical Network amid Child abuse Scandal." *Washington Post*, May 19, 2014. https://www.washingtonpost.com/national/religion/megachurch-pastors-leave-reformed-evangelical-network-amid-child-abuse-scandal/2014/05/19/abde8548-df8d-11e3-9442-54189bf1a809_story.html.
Balmer, Randall. *Evangelicalism in America*. Waco, TX: Baylor University Press, 2016.

BIBLIOGRAPHY

Barna, George. *Marketing the Church.* Colorado Springs, CO: Navpress, 1988.

———. *Revolution: Finding Vibrant Faith beyond the Walls of the Sanctuary.* Carol Stream, IL: Tyndale House, 2005.

Barth, Karl. *Church Dogmatics: The Doctrine of Creation,* Vol. 3 Part 4. Translated by G. W. Bromiley and T. F. Torrance. Edinburgh: T&T Clark, 2004.

Bartkowski, John P. *The Promise Keepers: Servants, Soldiers, and Godly Men.* New Brunswick, NJ: Rutgers University Press, 2003.

Baudrillard, Jean. *The Ecstasy of Communication.* New York: Semiotext(e), 2012.

Bauman, Zygmunt. *Liquid Modernity.* Cambridge: Polity, 2000.

Beaty, Katelyn. "Behind the Rise of Evangelical Women 'Influencers.'" *Religion & Politics,* December 10, 2019. https://religionandpolitics.org/2019/12/10/behind-the-rise-of-evangelical-women-influencers/.

Bebbington, David W. *Evangelicalism in Modern Britain: A History from the 1730s to the 1980s.* London: Unwin Hyman, 1989.

Bell, Matthew. "'The Biggest Megachurch on Earth and South Korea's 'Crisis of Evangelism.'" *Public Radio International,* May 1, 2017. https://www.pri.org/stories/2017-05-01/biggest-megachurch-earth-facing-crisis-evangelism.

Blair, Leonardo. "Megachurch Founder James MacDonald Allegedly Sought Murder for Hire, Police Investigating." *Christian Post,* May 20, 2019. https://www.christianpost.com/news/megachurch-founder-james-macdonald-allegedly-sought-murder-for-hire-police-investigating.html.

Bloch, Ernst. *Atheism in Christianity.* Translated by J. T. Swann. New York: Verso, 2009.

Bonhoeffer, Dietrich. *Discipleship.* Dietrich Bonhoeffer Works, vol. 4. Edited by Barbara Green and Reinhard Krauss. Minneapolis: Fortress, 2001.

Bosesveld, Sarah. "Q&A with Michael Pearl." *National Post,* November 12, 201. https://nationalpost.com/news/qa-with-michael-pearl.

Bote, Joshua. "He Wrote the Christian Case against Dating. Now He's Splitting from His Wife and Faith." *USA Today,* July 29, 2019. https://amp.usatoday.com/amp/1857934001.

Bourdieu, Pierre. *Distinction: A Social Critique of the Judgement of Taste.* London: Routledge, 1984.

———. "The Forms of Capital." In *Handbook of Theory of Research for the Sociology of Education,* 241–58. Santa Barbara, CA: Greenwood, 1986.

Bowler, Kate. *The Preacher's Wife: The Precarious Power of Evangelical Women Celebrities.* Princeton, NJ: Princeton University Press, 2019. Kindle version.

Briggs, Megan. "Beth Moore: Complementarianism Is Like an Abused Women." *Church Leaders,* October 4, 2019. https://churchleaders.com/news/363326-beth-moore-complementarianism-is-like-an-abused-woman.html.

Brueggemann, Walter. *Deep Memory, Exuberant Hope.* Minneapolis: Augsburg Fortress, 2000.

———. *Genesis.* Interpretation: A Bible Commentary for Teaching and Preaching. Atlanta: John Knox, 1982.

———. *Truth Speaks to Power: The Countercultural Nature of Scripture.* Louisville: Westminster John Knox, 2013.

Bruce, Steve. *PRAY TV: Televangelism in America.* New York: Routledge, 1990.

Bruinius, Harry. "Churches Struggle with their #MeToo Moment." *Christian Science Monitor,* April 20, 2018. https://www.csmonitor.com/USA/Politics/2018/0420/Churches-struggle-with-their-MeToo-moment.

BIBLIOGRAPHY

Burek, Josh. "Christian Faith: Calvinism Is Back." *The Christian Science Monitor*, March 27, 2010. https://www.csmonitor.com/USA/Society/2010/0327/Christian-faith-Calvinism-is-back.

Burke, Louise. "The #MeToo Shockwave: How the Movement Has Reverberated around the World." *The Telegraph*, March 9, 2018. https://www.telegraph.co.uk/news/world/metoo-shockwave/.

Burton, Tara Isabella. "Disgraced An Evangelical Leader Stripped of His Title. It's a Huge Moment for #MeToo." *Vox*, March 31, 2018. https://www.vox.com/2018/5/9/17332524/paige-patterson-sbc-metoo-evangelical.

Bushnell, Katharine C. *Dr. Katharine C. Bushnell: A Brief Sketch of Her Life Work*. Hertford: Rose & Sons, 1932.

Byers, Andrew. *TheoMedia: The Media of God and the Digital Age*. Eugene, OR: Cascade, 2013.

Byrd, Aimee. "#BillHybelsToo?" *First Things*, April 25, 2018. https://www.firstthings.com/web-exclusives/2018/04/billhybelstoo.

Cabasilas, Nicholas. *The Life in Christ*. Translated by Carmino J. Decatanzaro. Crestwood, NY: Saint Vladimir's Seminary Press, 1974.

Carpenter, Joel. "Contemporary Evangelicalism and Mammon." In *More Money, More Ministry: Money and Evangelicals in Recent North American History*, edited by Larry Eskridge and Mark Noll, 399–405. Grand Rapids: Eerdmans, 2000.

———. *Revise Us Again: The Reawakening of American Fundamentalism*. New York: Oxford University Press, 1997.

Carson, Don A., et al. "Why We Have Been Silent about the SGM Lawsuit." The Gospel Coalition, May 24, 2013. https://www.thegospelcoalition.org/article/why-we-have-been-silent-about-the-sgm-lawsuit/.

Carter, Joe. "Five Facts about Persecuted Chinese Pastor Wang Yi." Ethics and Religious Liberty Commission of the Southern Baptist Convention, December 21, 2018. https://erlc.com/resource-library/articles/5-facts-about-persecuted-chinese-pastor-wang-yi

———. "Persecuted Chinese Pastor Issues a 'Declaration of Faithful Disobedience.'" The Gospel Coalition, December 17, 2018. https://www.thegospelcoalition.org/article/persecuted-chinese-pastor-issues-declaration-faithful-disobedience/.

Caughey, Chris, and Crawford Gribben. "History, Identity Politics, and the 'Recovery of the Reformed Tradition.'" In *On Being Reformed: Debates over a Theological Identity*, edited by Matthew C. Bingham, et al., 1–26. New York: Palgrave MacMillan, 2018.

Chan, Francis. *Letters to the Church*. Colorado Springs, CO: David C Cook, 2019.

Chandler, Russell. "Test-Marketing the Gospel—A Consumer Survey Helped Design Willow Creek Church for Its 'Consumers.'" *San Francisco Chronicle*, December 24, 1989.

Chapman, Jennie. "Tender Warriors: Muscular Christians, Promise Keepers, and the Crisis of Masculinity in Left Behind." *Journal of Religion and Popular Culture* 21 (3) Fall 2009, 6–32.

Cheng, June. "House Church on a Hill." *World*, April 15, 2016. https://world.wng.org/2016/04/house_church_on_a_hill.

Chiaramonte, Perry. "Martyr Killed by Bulldozer Becomes Symbol of Growing Persecution of Christians in China." *Fox News*, April 22, 2016. www.foxnews.com/world/martyr-killed-by-bulldozer-becomes-symbol-of-growing-persecution-of-christians-in-china.

BIBLIOGRAPHY

Cho, David. "The Business of Filling Pews: Congregations Employ Marketing Consultants to Step Up Appeal." *The Washington Post*, March 6, 2005.

Choi, Peter. *George Whitefield: Evangelist for God and Empire*. Grand Rapids: Eerdmans, 2018.

Chow, Alexander. "Calvinist Public Theology in Urban China Today." *International Journal of Public Theology* 8:2 (2014) 158–75.

Chung, Jiyoung. "I Learned That the Happiness of the Father Leads to the Happiness of the Family, and the Happiness of the Company." Donga newspaper, June 4, 2012. http://news.donga.com/3/all/20120603/4673324/1.

"Churches Need to Act on Claims of Abuse." *South China Morning Post*, June 30, 2018. https://www.scmp.com/comment/insight-opinion/article/2153195/churches-need-act-claims-abuse.

Clark, Lynn Schofield. *From Angels to Aliens: Teenagers, the Media, and the Supernatural*. New York: Oxford University Press, 2003.

"Clinton Sought Guidance from Man of God Monthly." *Washington Times*, January 21, 1997.

Coleman, James S. *Foundations of Social Theory*. Cambridge, MA: Harvard University Press, 1990.

———. *The Globalization of Charismatic Christianity: Spreading the Gospel of Prosperity*. New York: Oxford University Press, 2000.

Connell, R. W. "Change among the Gatekeepers: Men, Masculinities, and Gender Equality in the Global Arena." *Signs* 30 (2005) 1801–25.

Cooperman, Alan. "Minister Admits to Buying Drugs and Massage." *The Washington Post*, November 4, 2006. https://www.washingtonpost.com/archive/politics/2006/11/04/minister-admits-to-buying-drugs-and-massage/193786b4-8322-4a1e-a6f6-bec7b08e6465/.

Corcoran, Katie E., and James K. Wellman, Jr. "'People Forget He's Human': Charismatic Leadership in Institutionalized Religion." *Sociology of Religion: A Quarterly Review* 77:4 (2016) 309–32.

Cox, Harvey. *Religion in the Secular City: Toward a Postmodern Theology*. New York: Simon and Schuster, 1984.

Crouch, Andy. *Playing God: Redeeming the Gift of Power*. Downers Grove, IL: InterVarsity, 2013.

———. "It's Time to Reckon with Celebrity Power." The Gospel Coalition, March 24, 2018. https://www.thegospelcoalition.org/article/time-reckon-celebrity-power/.

Dawson, Lorne L. *Comprehending Cults: The Sociology of New Religious Movements*. New York: Oxford University Press, 2006.

Dean, J. "Communicative Capitalism: Circulation and the Foreclosure of Politics." *Cultural Politics*, 1:1 (2005) 51–74.

DeGroat, Chuck. *When Narcissism Comes to Church: Healing Your Community from Emotional and Spiritual Abuse*. Downers Grove, IL: InterVarsity, 2020. Kindle book.

DeMuth, Mary. *We Too: How the Church Can Respond Redemptively to the Sexual Abuse Crisis*. Eugene, OR: Harvest House, 2019.

Denker, Angela. *Red State Christians: Understanding the Voters Who Elected Donald Trump*. Minneapolis: Fortress, 2019.

Devine, Daniel James. "Mahaney, Harris Leave Gospel Coalition Council." *World*, May 19, 2014. https://world.wng.org/2014/05/mahaney_harris_leave_gospel_coalition_council.

BIBLIOGRAPHY

———. "Not Bluffing." *World*, October 18, 2013. https://world.wng.org/2013/10/not_bluffing.

DeYoung, Rebecca Konyndyk. *Vainglory: The Forgotten Vice*. Grand Rapids: Eerdmans, 2014.

Dias, Elizabeth. "Her Evangelical Megachurch Was Her Hold. Then Her Daughter Said She Was Molested by a Minister." *The New York Times*, June 10, 2019. https://www.nytimes.com/2019/06/10/us/southern-baptist-convention-sex-abuse.html.

———. "Inside the Investigation into Child Sexual Abuse at Sovereign Grace Ministries." *Time*, February 16, 2016. https://time.com/4226444/child-sex-abuse-evangelical-church/.

DiMaggio, Paul. "Cultural Capital and School Success." *American Sociological Review* 47:2 (2005) 189–201.

Do, Anh. "Rick Warren's Saddleback Church Hosts Rwanda President, Spurring Outcry." *Los Angeles Times*, April 14, 2019. https://www.latimes.com/local/lanow/la-me-ln-rick-warren-saddleback-church-rawanda-president-20190414-story.html.

Donovan, Brian. "Political Consequences of Private Authority: Promise Keepers and the Transformation of Hegemonic Masculinity." *Theology and Society*, 27:6 (December, 1998) 817–43.

Downen, Robert, et al. "Abuse of Faith: 20 Years, 700 Victims: Southern Baptist Sexual Abuse Spreads as Leaders Resist Reforms." *The Houston Chronicle*, February 10, 2019. https://www.houstonchronicle.com/news/investigations/article/Southern-Baptist-sexual-abuse-spreads-as-leaders-13588038.php.

Doyle, Wright. "A Missed Opportunity: The Failure of A Bold Project." Global China Center, May 6, 2020. https://www.globalchinacenter.org/analysis/a-missed-opportunity-the-failure-of-a-bold-project.

Drane, John. *The McDonaldization of the Church: Consumer Culture and the Church's Future*. Macon, GA: Smyth & Helwys, 2001.

Dreher, Rod. "Kill Your Megachurch Worship." *The American Conservative*, January 14, 2016. https://www.theamericanconservative.com/dreher/kill-your-megachurch-worship/

Driscoll, Mark. *A Call to Resurgence*. Carol Stream, IL: Tyndale House, 2013.

Du Mez, Kristin. *Jesus and John Wayne: How White Evangelicals Corrupted a Faith and Fractured a Nation*. New York: Liveright, 2020.

———. *A New Gospel for Women: Katharine Bushnell and the Challenge of Christian Feminism*. New York: Oxford University Press, 2015.

Duduit, Michael. "The 25 Most Influential Pastors of the Past 25 Years." *Preaching Magazine* (2019). https://www.preaching.com/articles/the-25-most-influential-pastors-of-the-past-25-years/.

Eagle, David E. "Historicizing the Megachurch." *Journal of Social History* 48:3 (2015) 589–604.

Eckholm, Erik. "Preaching Virtue of Spanking, Even as Deaths Fuel Debate." *New York Times*, November 6, 2011. https://www.nytimes.com/2011/11/07/us/deaths-put-focus-on-pastors-advocacy-of-spanking.html?hp.

"Editorial: The Shameful Reality of South Korean Protestant Megachurches." *Hani.co.kr*, October 26, 2017. http://english.hani.co.kr/arti/english_edition/english_editorials/816201.html.

Einstein, Mara. *Brands of Faith: Marketing Religion in a Commercial Age*. New York: Routledge, 2007.

BIBLIOGRAPHY

Elisha, Omri. *Moral Ambition: Mobilization and Social Outreach in Evangelical Megachurches*. Oakland, CA: University of California Press, 2011.

Ellingson, Stephen. "New Research on Megachurches, Non-denominationalism and Sectarianism." In *Blackwell Companion to the Sociology of Religion*, edited by B. Turner, 447–66. Blackwood: Blackwell, 2010.

———. "Packaging Religious Experience, Selling Modular Religion: Explaining the Emergence and Expansion of Megachurches." In *Religion in Consumer Society: Brands, Consumers and Markets*, edited by François Gauthier and Tuomas Martikainen, 59–74. Surrey: Ashgate, 2013.

Ellul, Jacques. *Jesus and Marx: From Gospel to Ideology*. Eugene, OR: Wipf and Stock, 1988.

———. *Presence of the Kingdom*. New York: Seabury, 1967.

———. *Propaganda: The Formation of Men's Attitudes*. New York: Vintage, 1965.

———. *The Subversion of Christianity*. Eugene, OR: Wipf and Stock, 2011.

———. *The Technological Society*. New York: Vintage, 1964.

Elsbach, K. D. "Managing Organizational Legitimacy in the California Cattle Industry: The Construction and Effectiveness of Verbal Accounts." *Administrative Science Quarterly*, 39:1 (1994) 57–88.

Evans, Rachel Held. "The Abusive Teachings of Michael and Debi Pearl." A blog article, March 23, 2013. https://rachelheldevans.com/blog/the-abusive-teachings-of-michael-and-debi-pearl.

Everhart, Ruth. *The #MeToo Reckoning: Facing the Church's Complicity in Sexual Abuse and Misconduct*. Downers Grove, IL: InterVarsity, 2020.

———. "Women of the Bible Say #MeToo." *Christian Century*, July 17, 2018. https://www.christiancentury.org/article/critical-essay/women-bible-say-metoo.

"Ex PTL Employee Testifies He Had Sex with Bakker." *The Washington Post*, September 22, 1988.

FitzGerald, Frances. *The Evangelicals: The Struggle to Shape America*. New York: Simon and Schuster, 2017.

Flake, Carol. *Redemptorama: Culture, Politics, and the New Evangelicalism*. New York: Anchor, 1984.

Foucault, Michel. *Security, Territory, Population: Lectures at the Collège de France, 1977–78*. Translated by Graham Burchell. New York: Palgrave Macmillan, 2007.

"Foundation Documents." The Gospel Coalition. https://www.thegospelcoalition.org/about/foundation-documents/.

Freud, S. "On Narcissism: An Introduction." In *The Standard Edition of the Complete Psychological Works of Sigmund Freud*, Volume XIV (1914–1916): *On the History of the Psycho-Analytic Movement, Papers on Metapsychology and Other Works*, 67–102. London: Hogarth Press, 1994.

Fukuyama, Francis. *Trust: The Social Virtues and the Creation of Prosperity*. London: Hamish Hamilton, 1995.

Fulton, Brent. "The Church in China Today." Udemy.com, February, 2017. www.udemy.com/the-church-in-china-today/.

———. "Is There a Campaign Against Christianity in China?" *ChinaSource*, August 22, 2014). www.chinasource.org/resource-library/blog-entries/is-there-a-campaign-against-christianity-in-china.

Gafney, Wil. "Crucifixion and Sexual Violence." *Huffington Post*, March 28, 2018. https://www.huffpost.com/entry/crucifixion-and-sexual-violence_b_2965369.

BIBLIOGRAPHY

Gallagher, Sally K., and Sabrina L. Wood. "Godly Manhood Going Wild?: Transformations in Conservative Protestant Masculinity." *Sociology of Religion* 66:2 (2005) 135–60.
Galli, Mark. "Trump Should Be Removed from Office." *Christianity Today*, December 19, 2019. https://www.christianitytoday.com/ct/2019/december-web-only/trump-should-be-removed-from-office.html
Garrard-Burnett, Virginia, et al. *The Cambridge History of Religions in Latin America*. New York: Cambridge University Press, 2015.
Giddens, Anthony. *The Consequences of Modernity*. Cambridge: Polity, 1990.
———. *Modernity and Self-Identity: Self and Society in the Late Modern Age*. Cambridge: Polity, 1991.
Gifford, P. *Ghana's New Christianity: Pentecostalism in a Globalizing African Economy*. Indianapolis: Indiana University Press, 2004.
Gladwell, Malcolm. "The Cellular Church: How Rick Warren's Congregation Grew." *The New Yorker*, September 4, 2005. https://www.newyorker.com/magazine/2005/09/12/the-cellular-church.
Goodstein, Laurie. "He's a Superstar Pastor. She Worked for Him and Says He Groped Her Repeatedly." *The New York Times*, August 5, 2018. https://www.nytimes.com/2018/08/05/us/bill-hybels-willow-creek-pat-baranowski.html.
Graham, Ruth. "How a Megachurch Melts Down." *The Atlantic*, November 7, 2014. https://www.theatlantic.com/national/archive/2014/11/houston-mark-driscoll-megachurch-meltdown/382487/?single_page=true.
Green, Emma. "The Tiny Blond Bible Teacher Taking on the Evangelical Political Machine." *The Atlantic*, October, 2018. https://www.theatlantic.com/magazine/archive/2018/10/beth-moore-bible-study/568288/.
Griffiths, Mark. "Why We Seek the High of Stardom." *Psychology Today*, March 24, 2014. https://www.psychologytoday.com/us/blog/in-excess/201403/why-we-seek-the-high-stardom.
Griswold, Eliza. "Silence Is Not Spiritual: The Evangelical #MeToo Movement." *The New Yorker*, June 15, 2018. https://www.newyorker.com/news/on-religion/silence-is-not-spiritual-the-evangelical-metoo-movement.
Guinness, Os. *Dining with the Devil: The Megachurch Movement Flirts with Modernity*. Grand Rapids: Hourglass, 1993.
———. "Sounding Out the Idols of the Church Growth Movement." In *No God but God*, edited by Os Guinness and John Seel, 152–72. Chicago: Moody, 1992.
Hadden, Jeffery K. "The Globalization of American Televangelism." *International Journal of Frontier Missions* 7 (1990) 1.
———. "The Rise and Fall of American Televangelism." *Annals of the American Academy of Political and Social Science*, vol. 527, Religion in the Nineties (May, 1993) 113–30.
Hadden, Jeffery K., and A. Shupe. *Televangelism: Power and Politics on God's Frontier*. New York: Henry Holt, 1988.
Hadden, Jeffery K., and C. E. Swann, *Prime Time Preachers: The Rising Power of Televangelism*. Reading, MA: Addison-Wesley, 1981.
Hafiz, Yasmine. "Protesters Call for Pastor Mark Driscoll's Resignation after Multiple Scandals at Mars Hill Church." *The Huffington Post*, August 5, 2014. https://www.huffpost.com/entry/pasotr-mark-driscoll-resign_n_5651088.
Han, Ju Hui Judy. *Contemporary Korean/American Evangelical Missions: Politics of Space, Gender, and Difference*. PhD diss., University of California at Berkeley, 2009.

BIBLIOGRAPHY

Hansen, Colin. "Young, Restless, and Reformed." *Christianity Today*, September 22, 2006. https://www.christianitytoday.com/ct/2006/september/42.32.html.

———. *Young, Restless, Reformed: A Journalist's Journey with the New Calvinists*. Wheaton, IL: Crossway, 2008.

Harris, Joshua. "'I Kissed Dating Goodbye' Author: How and Why I Rethought Dating and Purity Culture." *USA Today*, November 23, 2018. https://www.usatoday.com/story/opinion/voices/2018/11/23/christianity-kissed-dating-goodbye-relationships-sex-book-column/2071273002/.

Harris, Paul. "Ted Haggard, Megachurch Founder Felled by Sex Scandal, Returns to Pulpit." *The Guardian*, June 5, 2010. https://www.theguardian.com/world/2010/jun/06/us-gay-scandal-pastor-church.

Hauerwas, Stanley. *Christian Existence Today: Essays on Church, World, and Living in Between*. Grand Rapids: Brazos, 1988.

Hauerwas, Stanley, and William H. Willimon. *Resident Aliens: A Provocative Christian Assessment of Culture and Ministry for People Who Know That Something Is Wrong*. Nashville: Abingdon, 1989.

Hayes, Kevin. "Is Conservative Christian Group, No Greater Joy Ministries, Pushing Parents to Beat Kids to Death?" *CBS News*, March 1, 2010. https://www.cbsnews.com/news/is-conservative-christian-group-no-greater-joy-ministries-pushing-parents-to-beat-kids-to-death/.

Heath, Elaine. *Healing the Wounds of Sexual Abuse: Reading the Bible with Survivors*. Grand Rapids: Brazos, 2019.

———. *We Were the Least of These: Reading the Bible with Survivors of Sexual Abuse*. Grand Rapids: Brazos, 2011.

Held, Shai. "The Babel Story Is about the Dangers of Uniformity." *Christian Century*, October 24, 2017. https://www.christiancentury.org/article/critical-essay/the-babel-story-is-about-dangers-uniformity.

Hendershot, Heather. *Shaking the World for Jesus: Media and Conservative Evangelical Culture*. Chicago: University of Chicago Press, 2004.

"Hereditary Succession at Myungsung Church Thwarted." *The Korea Bizwire*, September 14, 2018. http://koreabizwire.com/hereditary-succession-at-myungsung-church-thwarted/124441.

Hoffer, Eric. *The True Believer: Thoughts on the Nature of Mass Movements*. New York: Harper & Row, 1951.

Holifield, E. Brooks. *Theology in America: Christian Thought from the Age of the Puritans to the Civil War*. New Haven, CT: Yale University Press, 2003.

Hong, Yong-Gi. "Encounter with Modernity: The 'McDonaldization' and 'Charismatization' of Korean Mega-Churches." *International Review of Mission* 92:365 (2009) 239–55.

Horton, Greg. "How Calvinism Is Dividing the Southern Baptist Convention." *HuffPost*, June 6, 2013. https://www.huffpost.com/entry/how-calvinism-is-dividing-the-southern-baptist-convention_n_3399504.

Horton, Michael S. "The Church after Evangelicalism." In *Renewing the Evangelical Mission*, edited by Richard Lints, 134–60. Grand Rapids: Eerdmans, 2013.

Hoselitz, Berthold F. "The Early History of Entrepreneurial Theory." *Explorations in Entrepreneurial History* 3 (1951) 193–220.

Huckabee, Tyler. "James MacDonald and the End of the Celebrity Pastor." *Relevant*, February 21, 2019. https://relevantmagazine.com/god/church/james-macdonald-and-the-end-of-the-celebrity-pastor/.

BIBLIOGRAPHY

Immergut, Matthew, and Mary Kosut. "Visualising Charisma: Representations of the Charismatic Touch." *Visual Studies* 29:3 (2014) 272–84.

"Inside the Most Powerful Church in South Africa." *The Independent*, June 21, 2010. https://static.independent.co.uk/s3fs-public/thumbnails/image/2010/06/21/00/397726.bin?w968.

Ioussouf, Raissa. "Why #MeToo Isn't Taking Off in West Africa." *BBC*, February 3, 2018. https://www.bbc.com/news/av/world-africa-42923129/why-metoo-isn-t-taking-off-in-west-africa#sa-link_location=story-body&intlink_from_url=https%3A%2F%2Fwww.bbc.com%2Fnews%2Fworld-africa-48825936&intlink_ts=1582292314056-sa.

James, J., and B. Shoesmith. *Hillsong, Benny Hinn and the Message of Health and Wealth: Looking at Technology and Religion.* Conference. Perth: Murdoch University, 2006.

James, Jonathan D. *McDonaldisation, Masala McGospel and Om Economics: Televangelism in Contemporary India.* Newbury Park, CA: Sage, 2010.

Jun, Alexander. "Five Lessons from Persecuted Christians in China." The Gospel Coalition, January 7, 2019. https://www.thegospelcoalition.org/article/5-lessons-persecuted-christians-china/.

Keel, Othmar. *The Symbolism of the Biblical World: Ancient Near Eastern Iconography and the Book of Psalms.* University Park, PA: Eisenbrauns, 2016.

Keller, Timothy, "Introducing the New City Catechism." Crossway, April 17, 2017. www.crossway.org/articles/introducing-the-new-city-catechism/.

———. "A Letter from Europe." *Redeemer City to City Newsletter*, December 27, 2018.

———. "A Vision to Reach the City." *Outreach*, October 24, 2012. https://outreachmagazine.com/interviews/4932-tim-keller-a-vision-to-reach-thecity.html.

Kidd, Thomas S. "China Sentences Pastor Wang Yi to Nine Years in Prison." The Gospel Coalition, December 30, 2019. https://www.thegospelcoalition.org/blogs/evangelical-history/china-sentences-pastor-wang-yi-nine-years-prison/.

———. *George Whitefield: America's Spiritual Founding Father.* New Haven, CT: Yale University Press, 2014.

Kim, Allen, and Karen Pyke. "Taming Tiger Dads: Hegemonic American Masculinity and South Korea's Father School." *Gender and Society* 29:4 (August 2015) 509–33.

Kimmel, Michael. *Misframing Men: The Politics of Contemporary Masculinities.* New Brunswick, NJ: Rutgers University Press, 2010.

King, Wayne. "Swaggart Says He Has Sinned: Will Step Down." *The New York Times*, February 22, 1988.

Klett, Leah MarieAnn. "John MacArthur Clarifies Views on Beth Moore, Women Preachers: 'Empowering Women Makes Weak Men.'" *Christian Post*, November 13, 2019. https://www.christianpost.com/news/john-macarthur-clarifies-views-on-beth-moore-women-preachers-empowering-women-makes-weak-men.html.

———. "Joshua Harris Says 'I Kissed Dating Goodbye' Will Be Discontinued, Apologizes for 'Flaws.'" *Christian Post*, October 23, 2018. https://www.christianpost.com/news/joshua-harris-says-i-kissed-dating-goodbye-will-be-discontinued-apologizes-for-flaws.html.

———. "Leading Pastors Discuss Dangers of 'Celebrity Culture' in Church, How Body of Christ Should Respond." *Christian Post*, November 17, 2018. https://www.christianpost.com/news/leading-pastors-discuss-dangers-celebrity-culture-church-how-body-of-christ-should-respond.html.

BIBLIOGRAPHY

Kleiven, Tormod. "Sexual Misconduct in the Church: What Is It About?" *Pastoral Psychology* 67 (2018) 277–89.

Klewes, Joachim, and Robert Wreschniok. *Reputational Capital: Building and Maintaining Trust in the 21st Century*. New York: Springer, 2010.

Kum, Nami. *The Gendered Politics of the Korean Protestant Right: Hegemonic Masculinity*. New York: Palgrave Macmillan, 2016.

Knowles, Francine. "Leader of Oak Brook Religious Group Resigns amid Sex Harassment Allegations." *Chicago Sun-Times*, July 17, 2014. https://chicago.suntimes.com/2016/6/24/18464661/oak-brook-religious-group-sued-over-sex-harassment-allegations.

Kwon, Lillian. "C. J. Mahaney Takes Leave Over Charges of Pride, Hypocrisy." *Christian Post*, July 11, 2011.

Kwon, Young In, and Kevin M. Roy. "Changing Social Expectations for Work and Family Involvement among Korean Fathers." *Journal of Comparative Family Studies* 2 (2007) 285–305.

Laderman, Gary. *Sacred Matters: Celebrity Worship, Sexual Ecstasies, the Living Dead, and Other Signs of Religious Life in the United States*. New York: New, 2009.

Lambert, Frank. "'Peddler in Divinity': George Whitefield and the Great Awakening, 1737–1745." *The Journal of American History* 77:3 (December 1990) 812–37.

Laporte, Nicole. "The Korean Dads' 12-Step Program." *New York Times*, May 6, 2011. https://www.nytimes.com/2011/05/08/magazine/mag-08Here-t.html.

Le Bon, Gustave. *The Crowd: A Study of the Popular Mind*. New York: Viking, 1960.

Leder, Arie C. "City and Altar Building in Genesis." *Old Testament Essays* 32:1 (2019) 58–83.

Lee, Morgan. "Megachurch Pastor Confesses to Protecting Child Molester for Years." *Christian Post*, May 16, 2014. https://www.christianpost.com/news/megachurch-pastor-confesses-to-protecting-child-molester-for-years-119877/

———. "My Larry Nassar Testimony Went Viral. But There's More to the Gospel Than Forgiveness." *Christianity Today*, January 31, 2018. https://www.christianitytoday.com/ct/2018/january-web-only/rachael-denhollander-larry-nassar-forgiveness-gospel.html.

Lee, Shayne, and Philip Luke Sinitiere. *Holy Mavericks: Evangelical Innovators and the Spiritual Marketplace*. New York: New York University Press, 2009.

Lee, Yoonjung, and Kijung Kang. "The Development of Father School Program for Multicultural Families." *Korean Home Management Association Journal* (2010) 223–37.

Levin, Matt. "Megachurches Spread across the World." *Houston Chronicle*, July 31, 2015. https://www.chron.com/life/houston-belief/article/Texas-megachurches-inspiring-gigantic-churches-6417808.php.

Lippmann, Walter. *Public Opinion How People Decide: The Role of News, Propaganda and Manufactured Consent in Modern Democracy and Political Elections*. New Brunswick, NJ: Transaction, 1998.

Litman, Barry R., and Elizabeth Bain. "The Viewership of Religious Television Programming: A Multidisciplinary Analysis of Televangelism." *Review of Religious Research* 30:4, in Memoriam: Barbara June Watts Hargrove (June, 1989) 329–43.

Louth, Andrew, Marco Conti, and Thomas C. Oden. *Ancient Christian Commentary on Scripture: Old Testament I, Genesis 1–11*. Vol. 1. Downers Grove, IL: InterVarsity, 2001.

BIBLIOGRAPHY

Lule, Jack. *Globalization and Media: Global Village of Babel*. Lanham, MD: Rowman & Littlefield, 2012.
Lyon, D. *Jesus in Disneyland: Religion in Postmodern Times*. Cambridge: Polity Blackwell, 2000.
Ma, Li. *The Chinese Exodus: Migration, Urbanism and Alienation in Contemporary China*. Eugene, OR: Pickwick, 2018.
———. *Religious Entrepreneurism in China's Urban House Churches: The Rise and Fall of Early Rain Reformed Presbyterian Church*. London: Routledge, 2019.
Ma, Li, and Jin Li. *Surviving the State, Remaking the Church: A Sociological Portrait of Christians in Mainland China*. Eugene, OR: Pickwick, 2017.
Mahdavi, Pardis. "How #MeToo Became a Global Movement." *Foreign Affairs*, March 6, 2018. https://www.foreignaffairs.com/articles/2018-03-06/how-metoo-became-global-movement.
Marsden, George. *Understanding Fundamentalism and Evangelicalism*. Grand Rapids: Eerdmans, 1991.
Martin, Rachel. "Former Evangelical Pastor Rethinks His Approach to Courtship." *National Public Radio*, July 10, 2016.
Marty, Martin. "Minichurch and Megachurch." *The Christian Century* (1990) 107.
———. "The Revival of Evangelicalism and Southern Religion." In *Varieties of Southern Evangelicalism*, edited by David E. Harrell, Jr., 7–59. Macon, GA: Mercer University Press, 1981.
———. "A Spiritual Revival, a Commercial Boom, and yet . . . ." *Publishers Weekly* February 13, 1978, 83.
Matthews, K. A. *Genesis 1–11:26*. Vol. 1A. Nashville: Broadman & Holman, 1996.
Maxwell, D. "Editorial." *Journal of Religion in Africa* 28:3 (1988) 255.
McAlister, Melani. *The Kingdom of God Has No Borders: A Global History of American Evangelicals*. New York: Oxford University Press, 2018.
McBride, Jennifer M. *The Church for the World: A Theology of Public Witness*. New York: Oxford University Press, 2012.
McDonnel, M., and B. King. "Keeping Up Appearances: Reputational Threat and Impression Management after Social Movement Boycotts." *Administrative Science Quarterly* 58:3 (2014) 387–419.
McLuhan, Marshall. *The Mechanical Bride: Folklore of Industrial Man*. London: Duckworth Overlook, 2011.
Menzie, Nicola. "CJ Mahaney Drops Out of 2014 Together for the Gospel Conference Due to Sovereign Grace Lawsuit." *Christian Post*, July 2, 2013. https://www.christianpost.com/news/cj-mahaney-drops-out-of-2014-together-for-the-gospel-conference-due-to-sovereign-grace-lawsuit-99252/.
Merritt, Jonathan. "The Gospel Coalition and How (Not) to Engage Culture." *Religion News*, June 6, 2016. https://religionnews.com/2016/06/06/the-gospel-coalition-and-how-not-to-engage-culture/.
Merton, Thomas. *Thoughts in Solitude*. New York: Farrar, Straus and Giroux, 1956.
Metaxas, Eric. "China's Pastors Challenge Communist Govt in Joint Statement, Pledging Obedience to Jesus." *CNS News*, September 25, 2018. www.cnsnews.com/commentary/eric-metaxas/chinesepastors-challenge-communist-govt-joint-statement-pledge-obedience.

BIBLIOGRAPHY

"#MeToo Complaints Rife in Hong Kong's Protestant Churches, as Victims Come Forward." *Radio Free Asia*, June 25, 2018. https://www.rfa.org/english/news/china/hongkong-churches-06252018161340.html.

Miller, Emily McFarian. "Misconduct Allegations against Willow Creek Founder Bill Hybels Are Credible, Independent Report Finds." *The Washington Post*, March 1, 2019. https://www.washingtonpost.com/religion/2019/03/01/independent-report-finds-allegations-against-willow-creek-founder-bill-hybels-are-credible/.

Mohamed, A., and W. Gardner. "An Exploratory Study of Interorganizational Defamation: An Organizational Impression and Management Perspective." *Organizational Analysis* 12:2 (2004) 129–45.

Moll, Rob. "Day of Reckoning: Church Smith and Calvary Chapel Face an Uncertain Future." *Christianity Today*, February 16, 2007. https://www.christianitytoday.com/ct/2007/march/7.53.html.

———. "Unaccountable at Calvary Chapel." *Christianity Today*, May 8, 2006. https://www.christianitytoday.com/ct/2006/mayweb-only/119-12.0.html.

Moltmann, Jürgen. *The Crucified God*. Minneapolis: Fortress, 2015.

Monroe, Phil. "Must Read: Diane Langberg on 'Trauma as a Mission Field.'" Musings of a Christian Psychologist, June 20, 2011. https://philipmonroe.com/2011/06/20/must-read-diane-langberg-on-trauma-as-a-mission-field/.

Mtshilibe, Mbulelo. "Fake Pastors and False Prophets Rock South African Faith." *BBC News*, March 14, 2019. https://www.bbc.com/news/av/world-africa-47541131/fake-pastors-and-false-prophets-rock-south-african-faith.

Mullen, Wade. *Impression Management Strategies used by Evangelical Organizations in the Wake of An Image-Threatening Event*. PhD diss., Capital Seminary and Graduate School, 2018.

Myong-sik, Kim. "Hereditary Succession of Ministries in Megachurches." *The Korean Herald*, November 22, 2017. http://www.koreaherald.com/view.php?ud=20171112 1000771.

Neff, David. "CTI's Modest Dynamic Duo." *Christianity Today*, March 14, 2007. https://www.christianitytoday.com/ct/2007/april/8.96.html.

Neill, S. *A History of Christianity in India: The Beginnings to AD 1707*. Cambridge: Cambridge University Press, 1984.

Nesch, Elliott. *Church of Tares: Purpose Drive, Seeker Sensitive, Church Growth and New World Order*. A documentary, 2012.

"The New Calvins: Tensions Inside One of America's Most Successful Churches." *The Economist*, October 7, 2010. https://www.economist.com/united-states/2010/10/07/the-new-calvins.

"The New Rebel Cry: Jesus Is Coming!" *Time*, June 21, 1971.

Niebuhr, Gustav. "Promise Keepers Still Draws Crowds." *The New York Times*, May 21, 2001. https://www.nytimes.com/2001/05/21/us/promise-keepers-still-draws-crowds.html.

"Nigerian Pastor Biodun Fatoyinbo Steps Aside over Rape Allegations." *BBC*, July 1, 2019. https://www.bbc.com/news/world-africa-48825936.

Noll, Mark. *The Rise of Evangelicalism: The Age of Edwards, Whitefield, and the Wesleys*. Downers Grove, IL: Intervarsity, 2003.

———. *The Scandal of the Evangelical Mind*. Grand Rapids: Eerdmans, 1995.

Oh, Dallan. "16% of Korean Families Geographically Separated Because of Work and Children's School Locations." *Seoul News*, May 15, 2009.

BIBLIOGRAPHY

O'Neill, John. *Plato's Cave: Desire, Power, and the Specular Functions of the Media*. New York: Ablex, 1991.
Oppenheimer, Mark. "Evangelicals Find Themselves in the Midst of a Calvinist Revival." *The New York Times*, January 3, 2014. https://www.nytimes.com/2014/01/04/us/a-calvinist-revival-for-evangelicals.html.
Ostling, Richard N. "Jim Bakker's Crumbling World." *Time*, December 19, 1988.
Park, Ki-bum. "Multicultural Father School Camps." Hidomin, December 15, 2014. http://m.dimon.com/news/articleview.html?idxno=254742.
Parke, Caleb. "Well-Known Christian Author, Purity Advocate, Renouces His Faith: 'I Hope You Can Forgive Me.'" Fox News, July 29, 2019. https://www.foxnews.com/faith-values/christian-author-joshua-harris-kissed-dating-goodbye-faith.
Pearl, Debi. "Debi Pearl Weighs In on the IBLP Situation." No Greater Joy, April 24, 2014. https://nogreaterjoy.org/2014/04/24/debi-pearl-weighs-iblp-situation/?utm_content=buffer9e226&utm_medium=social&utm_source=facebook.com&utm_campaign=buffer.
Phillips, Tom. "Brazilian Televangelist Tells Followers to Embark on Media 'Fast.'" *The Guardian*, July 28, 2011. https://www.theguardian.com/world/2011/jul/28/televangelist-media-fast-brazil.
Piper, John. "Does a Woman Submit to Abuse?" Ask Pastor John, September 1, 2009. https://www.youtube.com/watch?v=3OkUPc2NLrM.
———. "Sexual-Abuse Allegations and the Egalitarian Myth." A John Piper Interview, Desiring God ministry website, March 16, 2018. https://www.desiringgod.org/interviews/sex-abuse-allegations-and-the-egalitarian-myth.
Piper, John, and Wayne Grudem. *Recovering Biblical Manhood and Womanhood: A Response to Evangelical Feminism*. Wheaton, IL: Crossway, 1991.
Posner, Sarah. *Unholy: Why White Evangelicals Worship at the Altar of Donald Trump*. New York: Random House, 2020.
Post, Jerrold. "Narcissism and the Charismatic Leader-Follower Relationship." *Political Psychology* 7:4 (1986) 675.
"The Promise Keepers." *Time*, October 6, 1997. http://content.time.com/time/covers/0,16641,19971006,00.html.
"Promise Keepers Brings Ministry to Kemper Arena." *Omaha World-Herald*, September 15, 2000.
"Promise Keepers' Goals." *The Christian Science Monitor*, October 3, 1997. https://www.csmonitor.com/1997/1003/100397.edit.edit.1.html.
Putnam, Robert D. "Bowling Alone: America's Declining Social Capital." *Journal of Democracy* 6 (1995) 65–78.
———. *Bowling Alone: The Collapse and Revival of American Community*. New York: Simon and Schuster, 2000.
Quackenbush, Casey. "The Religious Community Is Speaking Out against Sexual Violence with #ChurchToo." *Time*, November 22, 2017. https://time.com/5034546/me-too-church-too-sexual-abuse/.
"Rachael Denhollander Discusses Sovereign Grace Scandal on the Story with Martha Maccalum." Fox News, March 16, 2018. https://www.youtube.com/watch?v=NeY_7O5BvD4.
Rah, Soong-Chan. *The Next Evangelicalism: Freeing the Church from Western Cultural Captivity*. Downers Grove, IL: InterVarsity, 2009.

BIBLIOGRAPHY

Reaves, Jayme R. "#MeToo Jesus: Naming Jesus as a Victim of Sexual Abuse." *International Journal of Public Theology* 13 (2019) 387–412.

"Report: Former Co-Host Fletcher Says Bakker Bisexual." *Associated Press,* December 5, 1988.

"Richest Pastors in the World." *Forbes,* July 8, 2019. https://thedailysblog.com/entertainment/richest-pastors-in-the-world/.

Riis, Ole, and Linda Woodhead. *A Sociology of Religious Emotion.* New York: Oxford University Press, 2010.

Ritzer, George. *The McDonaldization of Society.* Oaks, CA: Pine Forge, 1993.

Robert, Dana Lee. *Christian Mission: How Christianity Became a World Religion.* Malden, MA: Wiley-Blackwell, 2009.

Rocke, Kris, and Joel Van Dyke. *Geography of Grace: Doing Theology from Below.* Tacoma, WA: Street Psalms, 2012.

Rockwell, D., and D. C. Giles. "Being a Celebrity: A Phenomenology of Fame." *Journal of Phenomenological Psychology* 40 (2009) 178–210.

Rohr, Richard. *Immortal Diamond.* San Francisco: Jossey-Bass, 2013.

Roof, Wade Clark. *Spiritual Marketplace: Baby Boomers and the Remaking of American Religion.* Princeton, NJ: Princeton University Press, 1999.

Royal, Kathryn. "Journalist Guidelines and Media Reporting in the Wake of #MeToo." In *#MeToo and the Politics of Social Change,* edited by Bianca Fileborn and Rachel Loney-Howes, 217–34. New York: Palgrave Macmillan, 2019.

Salter, Michael. "Online Justice in the Circuit of Capital: #MeToo, Marketization and the Deformation of Sexual Ethics." In *#MeToo and the Politics of Social Change,* edited by Bianca Fileborn and Rachel Loney-Howes, 53–69. New York: Palgrave Macmillan, 2019.

Sang-Hun, Choe. "South Korean Church Leader Sentenced to Prison in #MeToo Movement." *The New York Times,* November 22, 2018. https://www.nytimes.com/2018/11/22/world/asia/south-korea-pastor-rape.html.

Sargeant, Kimon Howland. *Seeker Churches: Promoting Traditional Religion in a Nontraditional Way.* New Brunswick, NJ: Rutgers University Press, 2000.

Saroyan, Strawberry. "Christianity, the Brand." *The New York Times,* April 16, 2006. https://www.nytimes.com/2006/04/16/books/christianity-the-brand.html.

Sataline, Susan. "Strategy for Church Growth Splits Congregants." *Pittsburg Post-Gazette,* September 5, 2006. https://www.post-gazette.com/life/lifestyle/2006/09/05/Strategy-for-church-growth-splits-congregants/stories/200609050170.

Schaller, Lyle E. "Megachurch!" *Christianity Today,* March 11, 1990, 29–33.

Schmidt, Rosemarie, and Joseph F. Kess. *Television Advertising and Televangelism.* Amsterdam: John Benjamins, 1986.

Schmidt, William. "For Jim and Tammy Bakker, Excess Wiped Out a Rapid Climb to Success." *The New York Times,* May 16, 1987.

Schultze, Quentin J. *Christianity and the Mass Media in America: Toward a Democratic Accommodation.* Ann Arbor, MI: Michigan State University Press, 2003.

———. "Introduction." In *American Evangelicals and the Mass Media,* edited by Quentin J. Schultze, 1–7. Grand Rapids: Baker, 1990.

———. "Keeping the Faith: American Evangelicals and the Media." In *American Evangelicals and the Mass Media,* edited by Quentin J. Schultze, 23–45. Grand Rapids: Baker, 1990.

BIBLIOGRAPHY

———. *Televangelism and American Culture: The Business of Popular Religion.* Grand Rapids: Baker, 1991.
Schultze, Quentin, and Robert H. Woods, Jr., eds. *Understanding Evangelical Media: The Changing Face of Christian Communication.* Downers Grove, IL: InterVarsity, 2001.
Schumpeter, Joesph A. *Capitalism, Socialism and Democracy.* New York: Haper Collins, 2008.
Schuurman, Peter J. *The Subversive Evangelical: The Ironic Charisma of an Irreligious Megachurch.* Montreal: Mcgill-Queen's University Press, 2019.
Scott, Emily. "The Bible's #MeToo Problems." *The New York Times,* June 16, 2018. https://www.nytimes.com/2018/06/16/opinion/sunday/women-the-bible-metoo.html.
Scott, S. "Revisiting the Total Institution: Performative Regulation in the Reinventive Institution." *Sociology* 44 (2010) 213–31.
Schwartz, Tony. *Media: The Second God.* New York: Random House, 1981.
Serrano, Alfonso. "Evangelist: I Bought Meth from Gay Escort." *CBS News,* November 2, 2006. https://www.cbsnews.com/news/evangelist-i-bought-meth-from-gay-escort/.
Shapiro, Nina. "Racketeering Suit Claims Mark Driscoll Misused Mars Hill Donor Dollars." *Seattle Times,* February 29, 2016. https://www.seattletimes.com/seattle-news/mark-driscoll-accused-of-racketeering-at-mars-hill-church/.
Shellnutt, Kate, and Morgan Lee. "Mark Driscoll Resigns from Mars Hill." *Christianity Today,* October 15, 2014. https://www.christianitytoday.com/ct/2014/october-web-only/mark-driscoll-resigns-from-mars-hill.html.
———. "Sovereign Grace Disputes Rachael Denhollander's Remarks." *Christianity Today,* February 6, 2018. https://www.christianitytoday.com/news/2018/february/sovereign-grace-rachael-denhollander-sgm-abuse-ct-interview.html.
Sherwood, Harriet. "Author of Christian Relationship Guide Says He Has Lost His Faith." *The Guardian,* July 29, 2019. https://www.theguardian.com/world/2019/jul/29/author-christian-relationship-guide-joshua-harris-says-marriage-over.
Sider, Ronald. *The Scandal of the Evangelical Conscience: Why Are Christians Living Just Like the Rest of the World?* Grand Rapids: Baker, 2005.
———, ed. *The Spiritual Danger of Donald Trump: 30 Evangelical Christians on Justice, Truth and Moral Integrity.* Eugene, OR: Cascade, 2020.
"Silence Is Not Spiritual: The Evangelical #MeToo Movement." *The New Yorker,* June 15, 2018. https://www.newyorker.com/news/on-religion/silence-is-not-spiritual-the-evangelical-metoo-movement.
Sinay-Mosias, Claudia. "Narcissism and #MeToo." *The Medium,* January 31, 2018. https://medium.com/@Mosinay/narcissism-and-me-too-116d30e23dcc.
Sledge, Benjamin. "Together for the Go$pel: The Evangelical Network Protecting a High-Profile Preacher." *Medium,* January 4, 2018. https://gen.medium.com/together-for-the-go-pel-26a23116d46b.
Smidt, Corwin. *Pastors and Public Life: The Changing Face of American Protestant Clergy.* New York: Oxford University Press, 2016.
Smietana, Bob. "Accusing SBC of 'Caving,' John MacArthur Says of Beth Moore: 'Go Home.'" *Religion News,* October, 19, 2019. https://religionnews.com/2019/10/19/accusing-sbc-of-caving-john-macarthur-says-beth-moore-should-go-home/.
Smith, Christian. *American Evangelicalism: Embattled and Thriving.* Chicago: University of Chicago Press, 1998.
———. *Christian America? What Evangelicals Really Want.* Berkeley, CA: University of California Press, 2000.

BIBLIOGRAPHY

Smith, C. Christopher, and John Pattison. *Slow Church: Cultivating Community in the Patient Way of Jesus.* Downers Grove, IL: InterVarsity, 2014.

Smith, D., and L. Campos. "Christianity and Television in Guatemala and Brazil: The Pentecostal Experience." *Studies in World Christianity* 1 (2005) 11.

Smith, Samuel. "Promise Keepers to Relaunch Men's Ministry with First Stadium Rally in 20 Years." *Christian Post*, May 16, 2019. https://www.christianpost.com/news/promise-keepers-to-relaunch-mens-ministry-with-first-stadium-rally-in-20-years.html.

Sobolik, Chelsea Patterson, and Casey B. Hough. "Increasing Religious Persecution in China." Ethics and Religious Liberty Commission of the Southern Baptist Convention, January 22, 2020. https://erlc.com/resource-library/articles/increasing-religious-persecution-in-china.

"South Korea Church Scandals under Spotlight in New Film." *France24*, October 10, 2017. https://www.france24.com/en/20171020-south-korea-church-scandals-under-spotlight-new-film.

"South Korean Hostage Apologizes for Being Captured." *CBC News*, August 31, 2007. https://www.cbc.ca/news/world/south-korean-hostage-apologizes-for-being-captured-1.659296.

Stanley, Brian. *The Global Diffusion of Evangelicalism: The Age of Billy Graham and John Stott.* Downers Grove, IL: InterVarsity, 2013.

Stewart, Katherine. *The Power Worshippers: Inside the Dangerous Rise of Religious Nationalism.* New York: Bloomsbury, 2020.

Stevenson, Jill. *Sensational Devotion: Evangelical Performance in Twenty-First-Century America.* Ann Arbor, MI: University of Michigan Press, 2013.

Stone, Meighan, and Rachel Vogelstein. "Celebrating #MeToo's Global Impact." *Foreign Policy*, March 7, 2019. https://foreignpolicy.com/2019/03/07/metooglobalimpactinternationalwomens-day/.

Strickler, Laura. "Televangelists: Who's Accountable?" *CBS News*, January 29, 2008. https://www.cbsnews.com/news/televangelists-whos-accountable/.

Strong, Rachel Marie. "When Child Discipline Becomes Abuse." *Christianity Today*, October 17, 2011. https://www.christianitytoday.com/women/2011/october/when-child-discipline-becomes-abuse.html.

Strother, Jason. "The Rise of Café Churches in South Korea." *The Atlantic*, May 8, 2017. https://www.theatlantic.com/international/archive/2017/05/south-korea-christians-election/525606/.

Sung, S. "Familism in the IMF Period and Gender Identity Crisis." *Journal of Korean Feminism* 18 (1998) 75–91.

Swedberg, Richard. "The Social Science View of Entrepreneurship: Introduction and Practical Applications." In *Entrepreneurship: The Social Science View*, edited by Richard Swedberg, 7–45. New York: Oxford University Press, 2000.

Thumma, Scott, and Dave Travis. *Beyond Megachurch Myths: What We Can Learn from America's Largest Churches.* San Francisco: Jossey-Bass, 2007.

Thumma, Scott, et al. *Megachurches Today 2005.* http://hirr.hartsem.edu/org/faith_megachurches_research.html#research.

"Towers of Babel: Is There Such a Thing as a Skyscraper Curse?" *The Economist*, March 26, 2015. https://www.economist.com/finance-and-economics/2015/03/26/towers-of-babel.

BIBLIOGRAPHY

Tracy, Steven R., and Andy Maurer. "#MeToo and Evangelicalism: Shattering Myths about Sexual Abuse and Power." Evangelical Theological Society Annual Meeting, Denver, November 13, 2018.

Trainor, Michael. *The Body of Jesus and Sexual Abuse: How the Gospel Passion Narrative Informs a Pastoral Approach*. Eugene, OR: Wipf and Stock, 2015.

———. "Mark's Passion Narrative: A Story of Abuse and Failed Intimacy." *Compass: A Review of Topical Theology* 37:1 (2003) 42.

Trible, Phyllis. *Texts of Terror: Literary-Feminist Readings of Biblical Narratives*. Minneapolis: Fortress, 1984.

Trueman, Carl. "Kissing Christianity Goodbye." *First Things*, July 30, 2019. https://www.firstthings.com/web-exclusives/2019/07/kissing-christianity-goodbye.

———. "Mark Driscoll's Problems, and Ours: The Crisis of Leadership in American Evangelicalism." *First Things*, March 14, 2014. https://www.firstthings.com/web-exculsives/2014/03/mark-driscolls-problems-and-ours.

———. "The Nameless One." *Reformation21*, September 2009. http://www.reformation21.org/articles/the-nameless-one.php.

Tune, Tim. "Promise Keepers to Add Digital Reach, Local Touch." *Baptist News*, May 31, 2019. http://www.bpnews.net/53012/promise-keepers-to-add-digital-reach-local-touch.

Tuttle, Shea. *Exactly as You Are: The Life and Faith of Mister Rogers*. Grand Rapids: Eerdmans, 2019.

"Unity Can Only Exist as a Gift of God's Spirit." Piecedhearts.com, May 27, 2012. https://www.piercedhearts.org/benedict_xvi/homilies/2012/may_27_pentecost.html.

Vaca, Daniel. *Evangelicals Incorporated: Books and the Business of Religion in America*. Cambridge, MA: Harvard University Press, 2019.

Vala, Carsten. "Book Review: Religious Entrepreneurism in China's Urban House Churches: The Rise and Fall of Early Rain Reformed Presbyterian Church by Li Ma." Review of Religion and Chinese Society 7 (1) 149–52.

Van Biema, David. "The New Calvinism: Ten Ideas Changing the World Right Now." *Time*, March 26, 2009. http://content.time.com/time/specials/packages/article/0,28804,1884779_1884782_1884760,00.html.

Veale, Jennifer. "Korean Missionaries Under Fire." *Time*, July 27, 2007. http://content.time.com/time/world/article/0,8599,1647646,00.html.

Voegelin, Eric. *Modernity without Restraint*. In *The Collected Works of Eric Voegelin*, vol 5. Columbia, MO: University of Missouri Press, 1999.

———. *The New Science of Politics: An Introduction*. Chicago: The University of Chicago Press, 1987.

———. *Order and History*, vol. 1: *Israel and Revelation*. In *The Collected Works of Eric Voegelin*, vol. 14. Edited by Maurice P. Hogan. Columbia, MO: University of Missouri Press, 2001.

———. *Science, Politics and Gnosticism*. Wilmington, DE: Intercollegiate Studies Institute, 2005.

Von Rad, Gerhard. *Old Testament Theology Vol. 1: The Theology of Israel's Historical Traditions*. Translated by D. M. G. Stalker. New York: Harper & Row, 1962.

Wade, Matthew. "Seeker-Friendly: The Hillsong Megachurch as An Enchanting Total Institution." *Journal of Sociology* 52:4 (2016) 661–76.

Waltke, Bruce K. *Genesis: A Commentary*. Grand Rapids: Zondervan, 2001.

BIBLIOGRAPHY

Ward, David J. "The Lived Experience of Spiritual Abuse." *Mental Health, Religion & Culture* 14:9 (2011) 899–915.

Ward, Pete. *Celebrity Worship*. London: Routledge, 2019.

———. *Gods Behaving Badly: Media, Religion, and Celebrity Culture*. Waco, TX: Baylor University Press, 2011.

———. *Liquid Church*. Grand Rapids: Baker, 2001.

Warren, James. "Billy Graham's Troubling, Nasty Nixon Moment." *US News*, February 28, 2018. https://www.usnews.com/opinion/thomas-jefferson-street/articles/2018-02-28/dont-forget-billy-grahams-anti-semitic-turn-with-richard-nixon.

———. "Nixon, Graham Anti-Semitism on Tape." *The Chicago Tribune*, March 1, 2002. https://www.chicagotribune.com/news/ct-xpm-2002-03-01-0203010267-story.html.

Warren, Tish Harrison. *Liturgy of the Ordinary: Sacred Practices in Everyday Life*. Downers Grove, IL: InterVarsity, 2016. Kindle version.

Weber, Jeremy. "C. J. Mahaney, Joshua Harris Resign from Gospel Coalition after SGM Abuse Conviction." *Christianity Today*, May 19, 2014. https://www.christianitytoday.com/news/2014/may/c-j-mahaney-joshua-harris-resign-from-gospel-coalition-sgm.html.

Weber, Max. *Economy and Society: An Outline of Interpretive Sociology*. Edited by G. Roth and C. Wittich. Berkeley, CA: University of California Press, 1978.

———. *The Theory of Social and Economic Organization*. Translated by A. M. Henderson and T. Parsons. New York: Free, 1947.

Wehr, D. S. "Spiritual Abuse: When Good People Do Bad Things." In *The Psychology of Mature Spirituality*, edited by P. Young-Eisendrath and M. E. Miller, 47–61. London: Routledge, 2000.

Welch, Craig. "The Rise and Fall of Mars Hill Church." *Seattle Times*, September 13, 2014. https://www.seattletimes.com/seattle-news//2024534198_marshillprofilexml.html?mbaseid=2024534198.

Wellman, James K. *Rob Bell and the New American Christianity*. Nashville, TN: Abingdon Press, 2012.

Wenham, G. J. *Genesis 1–15*. Vol. 1. Dallas: Word, 1987.

Wiersbe, W. W. *Wiersbe's Expository Outlines on the Old Testament* (Gen 11:1–9). Wheaton, IL: Victor, 1993. Accessed on Logos Software.

Wignall, Ross. "A Man after God's Own Heart: Charisma, Masculinity and Leadership at a Charismatic Church in Brighton and Hove, UK." *Religion* 46:3 (2016) 389–411.

Wigger, John. *PTL: The Rise and Fall of Jim and Tammy Faye Bakker's Evangelical Empire*. New York: Oxford University Press, 2017.

Wong, Tessa. "Inside Singapore's City Harvest Megachurch Scandal." *BBC News*, October 21, 2015. https://www.bbc.com/news/world-asia-34589932.

Worthen, Molly. *Apostles of Reason: The Crisis of Authority in American Evangelicalism*. New York: Oxford University Press, 2013.

———. "Who Would Jesus Smack Down?" *The New York Times*, January 11, 2009. https://www.nytimes.com/2009/01/11/magazine/11punk-t.html.

Young, Nancy Beck. "How Franklin Graham Betrayed His Father's Legacy." *The Washington Post*, May 2, 2019. https://www.washingtonpost.com/outlook/2019/05/02/how-franklin-graham-betrayed-his-fathers-legacy/.

BIBLIOGRAPHY

Yue, Cai. "Only for Men: On America's Promise Keeper Movement." *Overseas Campus*, November 16, 2018. http://ocfuyin.org/oc24-12.

Žižek, Slavoj. *The Plague of Fantasies*. New York: Verso, 1997.

Zylstra, Sarah Eekhoff. "How Chinese Pastors Developed Their Theology for Suffering." The Gospel Coalition, April 22, 2020. https://www.thegospelcoalition.org/article/how-chinese-pastors-developed-their-theology-for-suffering/.

———. "Young, Restless, and Reformed in China." The Gospel Coalition, March 27, 2017. https://www.thegospelcoalition.org/article/young-restless-and-reformed-in-china/.

Index

Subject Index

accountability, 19, 51, 54, 62, 71, 77, 82, 97, 139
Africa, 4, 15, 98–99, 101, 103–4, 113, 125
Asia, 4, 15, 22, 98, 101, 103–4, 106–7, 113, 137

celebrity culture, 10, 52, 87
celebrity pastor, 10, 14, 20, 27, 30, 46–48, 52–54, 57, 60, 64, 71, 77, 82–83, 85, 93, 97, 111
charisma, charismatic, 6, 10, 14, 23, 25–27, 29, 34–37, 40–41, 49, 52–53, 62n16, 64, 70, 72, 74, 93, 100, 122, 132
communication, 3, 6, 8, 12, 14, 17, 19–20, 23, 27–28, 32–33, 35, 39, 42, 44, 52, 56, 58, 72, 77, 97, 107, 111, 129
conservative, conservatism, 9, 30, 33–34, 44, 47, 51, 66, 73, 79, 89–91, 101–3, 110, 138
consumerism, 10, 16, 20, 46, 53, 55, 63, 101, 120
corruption, 51, 60, 103, 106, 129,

entrepreneurism, entrepreneurship, 6–8, 14–17, 20, 22–23, 25, 27–29, 31–37, 39–41, 44, 51, 54, 57, 60, 66, 77, 83, 110, 120, 122, 135, 138
ethics, 11, 16, 18, 20, 31, 40, 80, 111–12, 121–22

evangelicalism, 4–9, 11, 16–21, 29, 32, 35, 38, 45–47, 53, 60, 65, 69, 71–72, 77–78, 81, 85, 88, 96, 98, 101–2, 104, 108, 117, 120–21, 130, 137

Global South, 95–96, 117
globalization, globalized, 3–4, 10, 12, 16–19, 96–98, 106, 113–17, 139
Gnosticism, gnostic, 34, 74

Jesus (Christ), 4, 6, 10, 16, 20, 39, 41, 56, 63, 71, 78, 86, 92, 117–18, 120, 123–30, 134–36

Latin America, 15, 98, 101
leadership, 3, 6, 12, 14, 17–18, 20, 22–27, 29, 36, 64–66, 78, 80, 83, 87, 89, 91–2, 96, 103, 109–111, 120, 133, 138–39

masculinity, 6, 9, 30, 65–67, 106–8
mass media, 7, 10, 13, 16–20, 28, 31, 33, 39, 44, 48–52, 62, 77, 82, 93, 97, 101, 116–17, 120–21, 133, 139
McDonaldization, 18, 32, 115
megachurch, 5–6, 8–9, 11, 17–18, 28–31, 46, 54, 57, 62–65, 69–73, 78–80, 83–84, 86, 92, 99–100, 102–4, 106, 134
missionary, 3, 50, 95–97, 105, 137–38
modernity, 20–21, 38, 49, 53, 73–74, 103, 115, 120, 130

161

narcissism, 7, 26, 51–55, 93, 133

New Calvinism, 9, 31, 68

pathology, pathological, 16, 20, 92
patriarchy, patriarchal, 6, 9, 11, 24, 52, 89, 103, 108
Promise Keepers, 9, 30, 40, 65–68, 106–8
public life, 4, 15, 51, 54–55, 92, 102
public square, 7, 10, 44, 60, 121
public theology, 124, 128

radical, 4, 105

sexual abuse, 4–6, 52, 81, 83, 87, 89–90, 94, 110–11, 114, 125–28, 138

technique 6–7, 10, 20, 22–25, 27–28, 31–32, 34–35, 37–38, 40–41, 44, 57, 59–63, 72, 74, 100, 107, 133
technology 6–7, 10, 20, 24, 28, 31, 33, 37, 43, 64, 73, 97, 115, 120–21
televangelism, 8–9, 11, 28–30–31, 33, 45, 50, 60–61, 65, 77, 98–102, 115
trauma, traumatic, 4, 124–25, 129, 136

urbanism, urbanization, 10, 12–13, 16, 20–21, 23

#MeToo, 4–5, 9–10, 17–20, 70, 80–82, 87–88, 90–93, 111, 113–15, 123–29, 136, 138–39
#ChurchToo, 5, 18–19, 87–88, 93, 115, 126–27, 136, 139

Author Index

Chuck DeGroat, 52, 54, 132
Corwin Smidt, 4, 54
Eric Voegelin, 11, 34, 74
George Marsden, 4n3
Jacques Ellul, 19, 23, 33, 74, 122–23
Joel Carpenter, 54–55
Kristin Du Mez, 6, 47, 55, 82, 92
Max Weber, 23, 25–26
Mark Noll 4, 60
Os Guinness, 32, 49, 64, 73, 130
Quentin Schultz, 28, 32, 35, 52, 77
Ronald Sider, 4

Scripture index

Genesis 11:1–9	10–11, 13, 22, 42–43, 58, 75–76, 95, 124
Philippians 2:1–11	20, 119, 124–25, 128
Judges 19	124, 126–28
Romans 13:13–14	131
Matthew 5:14–15	120
Matthew 6:5–6	120
Matthew 8:4	120
Mark 7:36	120

www.ingramcontent.com/pod-product-compliance
Lightning Source LLC
Chambersburg PA
CBHW030113170426
43198CB00009B/614